MASTERING THE ART *of*
EMBROIDERY

Appliqué, goldwork, and surface stitching worked on
Holland linen *by Sophie Long.*

MASTERING THE ART *of* EMBROIDERY

TUTORIALS, TECHNIQUES, *and* MODERN APPLICATIONS

SOPHIE LONG

CHRONICLE BOOKS
San Francisco

First published in the United States
in 2013 by Chronicle Books LLC.

Copyright © 2013 by RotoVision SA.

Library of Congress Cataloging-
in-Publication Data available.

ISBN: 978-1-4521-0963-3

Manufactured in China

Cover design: Hillary Caudle
Cover embroidery: Amanda Want
(Amandajwant@googlemail.com)
Art Director: Emily Portnoi
Art Editor: Jennifer Osborne
Design concept: rehabdesign
Layout: Lucy Parrisi
Illustrations: Rob Brandt

10 9 8 7 6 5 4 3 2 1

Chronicle Books LLC
680 Second Street
San Francisco, CA 94107
www.chroniclebooks.com

Hand embroidered using cotton embroidery floss on linen
by Jazmin Berakha.

CONTENTS

SECTION ONE
HAND EMBROIDERY

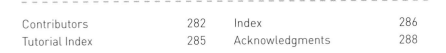

RESOURCES

INTRODUCTION

I have always had an interest in textiles. After studying Art and Textiles at school, I undertook a three-year apprenticeship in Embroidery at the Royal School of Needlework at Hampton Court Palace, UK. My love for embroidery and embellishments increased as I learned and perfected each technique to an extremely high standard. After the apprenticeship, I felt strongly that it was important to pass on this dying art form—and what better way to keep it alive than to teach it? The teaching of embroidery has taken me all over the world, passing on skills that are quite rare but have a surprising number of followers. Passing on my knowledge of embroidery gives me enormous joy, and the students are always appreciative. It is amazing to witness the spark of understanding in my students and watch as they create beautiful works of art. Writing a book was the natural next step toward reaching a wider audience to spread these skills and to showcase a range of extremely talented artists from around the world.

This book starts with the tools and materials you will need. Each chapter explains a different embroidery technique. Gallery pages display a range of exquisite examples of artists' work using that technique. An overview provides the history of the technique and details of its contemporary uses. The main part of the chapter consists of tutorials to guide you step by step through the different processes within each technique, along with illustrations. On these pages you will also find a list of materials and tips to help you to work in the most effective way. Each chapter features an artist, with details of the processes behind the artist's creation and superb photographs. I was truly inspired by all of the contemporary artists featured in this book and I hope this book will inspire you to pick up a needle to create your very own works of art.

1. Backstitch, satin stitch, and brick stitch using embroidery floss on cotton *by Melissa Crowe*.
2. Needlepoint using silk and ivory threads on canvas *by Heather Gray*.

TOOLS AND MATERIALS

There are a number of basic tools and materials that
you will need for the majority of embroidery techniques.
They are a good investment, and if looked after will
last a lifetime. Each tutorial will state what equipment
is needed for that stitch or technique. In Section Three,
you will find a list of suppliers that sell the
materials, threads, and equipment.

FRAMES

Whichever fabric you are working on, it is important to
keep it taut while stitching. A taut piece of fabric in a frame
ensures that the stitches are worked to a good tension.
There are a number of frames available, ranging in price
and size. The frame you use should be large enough for
the piece of work you are doing.

Slate frames are the recommended frame to use for
large or complex pieces. These come in a range of sizes;
the most common and versatile is a 24-in/61-cm frame.
With a slate frame, you need to stitch your desired fabric
into the frame. This enables you to get it as tight as possible.
The slate frame should then be placed on top of trestles
or balanced on suitable rests.

Hoop frames are also very useful, especially for smaller
pieces of embroidery, or for sampling stitches before
working them on the actual piece. These frames come
in a range of sizes. Some can be attached to a table
while others have a seat frame, which you can sit on and
therefore use in a range of surroundings. If you are using
a ring frame, it is a good idea to bind the edges using a strip
of cotton since this makes the fabric grip better in the
frame and prevents the hoop from marking the fabric.

FABRICS

The range of materials available is huge. For some
techniques, specific fabrics are traditionally used; in these
cases, they will be listed. When picking a fabric, think
about the design and the colors you will use—will they
work well together? You also need to consider its qualities.
Will the fabric support the weight of the embroidery?

If you are concerned that the fabric may not be strong
enough to support the embroidery, it can be backed onto
fine cotton. Frame up the cotton and then stitch the
chosen fabric onto that.

THREADS

There are huge ranges of threads now available; they all have their uses, depending on the technique you are working. For example, when working small, delicate pieces of stumpwork, you would often use one strand of stranded cotton. When working tent stitch on canvas, chunky wool would be more appropriate. As you go through this book, each tutorial will list the correct threads to use, but feel free to experiment with other threads.

Other useful equipment

Embroidery scissors Use only for threads, not for paper or fabric, which will blunt them

Tape measure

Propelling pencil or hard pencil that won't smudge

Thimble

Needles in a range of types

Tweezers for removing fluff and unpicking

Glass-headed pins

Iron Clean, so as not to leave marks

Fabric scissors

Goldwork scissors Metal threads blunt scissors so keep an old pair for goldwork

Stiletto for making holes in fabric without damaging the threads

Mellor This is a useful laying tool

Fine liner for drawing designs

Graph paper for creating designs

Tracing paper for creating designs

NEEDLES

You will need different needles, depending on the technique you are working with. When selecting which needle to use, make sure that the eye of the needle allows the thread to pass through without damaging it, but is not so big that the thread keeps slipping off. Within each section, the recommended needles will be stated.

Tapestry needles are blunt; you use them when you do not need to pierce the fabric because the holes are already provided. They are mostly used on counted thread work but are also useful to have for working woven stitches, because the blunt end does not catch on the spokes.

Chenille needles have large eyes with sharp points, so they can be used when the thread is quite thick.

Embroidery needles are small needles with sharp points that are used for surface embroidery when using fine threads.

Beading needles are very long and fine and used only for beadwork. The needle is fine enough to allow beads to pass onto it, while the length enables you to pass through a row of beads in one go.

Curved needles are semicircular with a point, which is very useful when working stitches in difficult-to-reach areas and for mounting work.

STARTING AND FINISHING

To achieve the best results, it is important to start and
finish all threads in the correct way. The best practice is
to avoid having excess thread and knots on the back of the
embroidery. If you mount the piece ready for framing,
excess knots will cause ripples and puckering in the fabric.

WASTE KNOT TECHNIQUE

To start a thread on a piece of surface embroidery,
the general rule is to tie a knot in the end of the thread.
However, there are times when this method is not
possible, for example on evenweave fabric, where there
will not be outlines that will cover these starting and
finishing stitches. Take the thread down, leaving the
knot on the surface of the fabric, either on a design line,
or within a design shape, which will later be covered with
embroidery. You then work two small stitches, again on the
line or within the design shape; these work as anchoring
stitches. Now you can cut off the knot.

To finish the thread, you bring the needle up on another
design line or design area not yet worked, and repeat
the two anchoring stitches. Bring the needle back up
to the top of the fabric, holding onto the thread, so that
the tension is tight. Get your scissors close to where the
thread comes out of the fabric, and cut it off.

COUNTED THREAD

When you are not using outlines or dense areas of
stitching, mostly with counted thread techniques,
for example, canvas blackwork, you can use a
different method.

To start a thread, put a knot in the end of the thread and
take the thread down, leaving the knot on top of the fabric,
approximately 1½ in/4 cm away from where you want
to work. Bring the needle up and work the stitches.
Work in the direction that the knot was placed, so that
your stitches catch in the thread, which is worked across
the back. Once you have worked back to the knot, check
that the thread on the back has been caught in with the
counted stitches. Pull on the knot to create tension,
and cut it off.

To finish the thread, bring the thread up farther along
the fabric, approximately 1½ in/4 cm from the stitches.
Leave the thread on the top and start off the new thread.
Work the stitches across the design, until you get to the
finished thread. You should have caught in the thread on
the back. Pull on the knot to create tension, and cut it off.
If it is not caught on the back, weave through some of the
stitches on the reverse.

SECTION ONE

HAND EMBROIDERY

Beading, free machine embroidery, and hand embroidery
using cotton and rayon sewing threads on buckram canvas
and cotton fabric *by Monika Kinner-Whalen.*

CHAPTER 1
SURFACE EMBROIDERY

Surface embroidery refers to any embroidery that
is worked straight onto the fabric using decorative
stitches and threads. The stitches are not counted,
so accuracy and precision are required to ensure that
the stitches are worked correctly to the correct tension
and length. Surface embroidery techniques can be
worked on their own or combined with others.

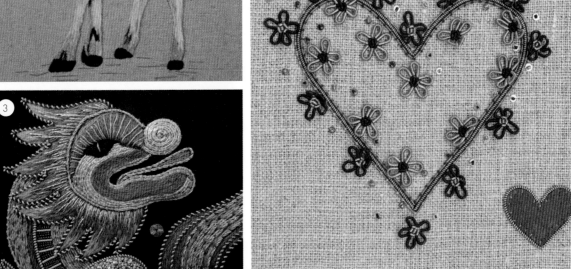

1. Natural silk shading of a giraffe worked in stranded cottons on a linen background *by Sophie Long.*
2. Natural silk shading of a lily worked in stranded cottons on a silk background *by Nicola Hooper.*
3. Goldwork dragon worked in a range of metal threads and stranded cottons, worked on a brown silk background *by Sophie Long.*
4. Goldwork heart worked in metal threads and kid leather on a linen background *by Sophie Long.*
5. Cherries worked in natural silk shading in stranded cottons on a silk background *by Rachel Doyle.*

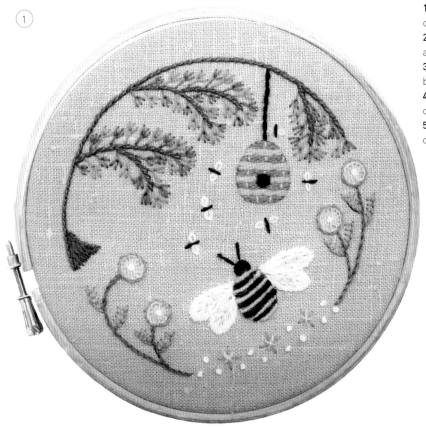

1

1. Crewelwork bee in crewel stitches worked on a linen background *by Emily Wilmarth*.
2. A combination of silk shading, goldwork, and appliqué worked on linen *by Lucy Barter*.
3. Kingfisher worked in silk shading on a linen background *by Trish Burr*.
4. Long and short stitch using stranded cottons on toast *by Judith Klausner* (photo by Steve Pomeroy).
5. Hand embroidered with stranded cottons on cotton *by Maricor Maricar*.

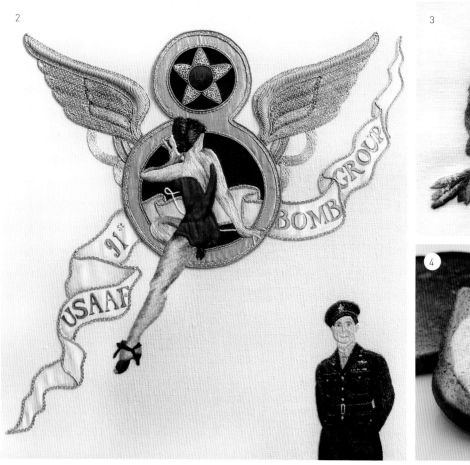

2

3

4

WE ARE THE MUSIC MAKERS & WE ARE THE DREAMERS OF DREAMS

1. Crewelwork cushion cover worked using stranded cottons on a linen fabric *by Hiromi Widerquist*.
2. Japanese camelia embroidered pendant worked on cotton in stranded cottons *by Hiromi Widerquist*.
3. Embroidered butterfly necklace worked on canvas in long and short stitch in stranded cottons *by Hiromi Widerquist*.
4. Embroidered door, created as part of a theater show, embroidered live on stage in embroidery thread, wool, rope, string, and lights worked on a wooden door *by Sarah Greaves* (photo by Dylan Chubb).

5

6

5. Natural silk shading of pansies worked on a linen background *by Trish Burr*.
6. Hand embroidered using stranded cottons on 100% cotton *by Bec Groves*.
7. Close-up of writing worked in split stitch in stranded cottons on a linen background *by Sophie Long*.

7

1. Hand embroidered using stranded cottons and floss on a homespun cotton *by Maricor Maricar.*
2. Diamond birthstone butterfly worked in silk shading in stranded cottons and Swarovski crystals on Thai silk *by Sarah Johnson.*

3. Hand embroidered using stranded cottons on 100% cotton *by Bec Groves.*

4. A combination of appliqué, goldwork, and surface stitching worked on a linen background, with a wired three-dimensional cord *by Sophie Long.*

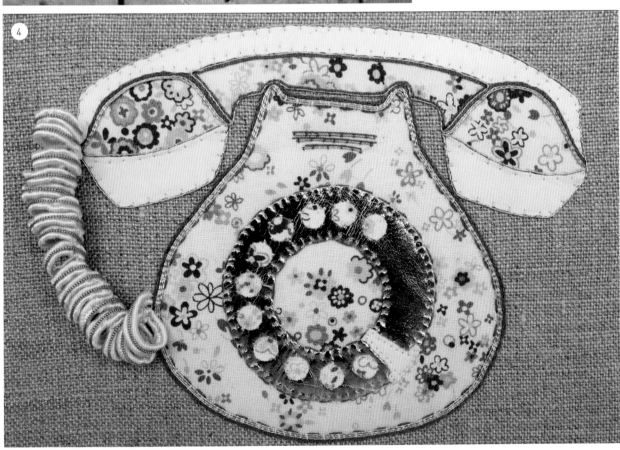

CREWELWORK

Crewel is an old Welsh word meaning "wool." Crewel embroidery is produced using wool rather than cotton or silk because it gives a much thicker and raised appearance to the finished piece. Crewel embroidery can be found on clothing, cushions, pillowcases, bags, and framed wall pieces.

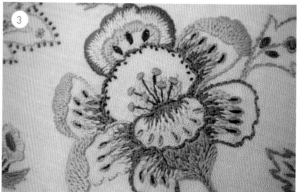

Crewel embroidery probably originated from the earliest Welsh spinners, who produced two-ply wool to decorate their clothing. Very early examples have not survived; the most famous one still in existence is the Bayeux Tapestry in Normandy, France, created in the 11th century.

In the Jacobean period (1603–25), crewelwork became popular for the decoration of domestic furnishings of large houses. Themes from the natural world of flora and fauna were embroidered on linen and cotton twill-weave fabrics. Embroidered jackets for both men and women were also popular. At this time, foreign traders brought brightly colored textiles incorporating designs of exotic birds and animals from the Far East to England. These fabrics were the inspiration for brightly colored designs; tree-of-life foliage designs were common. During the rest of the Stuart period (1603–1714), crewelwork reached the height of its popularity as young ladies took up this form of needlework as a hobby to create furnishings for their own homes.

In the following century, there was a surge of interest in paintings accompanied by the embroidery skill known as needle painting. Highly skilled needlewomen reproduced the detailed work of portraits using crewel wools.

Although crewel embroidery was traditionally made using highly twisted two-ply wool, modern embroiderers have an extensive choice of threads, including silk, mercerized cotton, and metal threads. With such a wide range of materials available, the traditional two-ply wool is now less popular. Nevertheless, the general stitches have stayed the same. Designs have developed over time as well, and although the tree of life is still a fairly common theme in crewelwork pieces, it has declined in popularity. Often pieces of embroidery worked in crewelwork stitches are referred to as free-style embroidery.

1. Jacobean crewelwork bird worked in crewel wools on linen twill *by Lizzy Lansberry.*
2. Crewelwork rooster worked using a range of wools on a linen twill background *by Mary Corbet.*
3. Crewelwork cushion cover worked using stranded cottons on a linen fabric *by Hiromi Widerquist.*
4. Surface embroidery worked using stranded cottons and perle on a white linen background *by Jo Avery.*
5. Crewelwork carnations worked in a range of wools on a vintage cotton and linen mix *by Eva-Maria Nerling.*

TRELLIS WORK
─●── TUTORIAL ──●─

This popular stitch is generally used for large areas because it can cover them fairly quickly. The basic trellis is a grid that can be worked in a range of different sizes. When starting and finishing a thread, make sure you do so on the design lines; you will work an outline stitch around your design once the trellis is complete.

Materials
- Fabric (any)
- Chenille or embroidery needle
- Thread
- Embroidery scissors

Step 1

Always start the bars in the middle of the shape because this helps to keep the grid even. Bring the needle up on the design line and take the needle down horizontally across to the opposite design line.

Step 2

Bring the needle up the desired distance above the first line. Take the needle down on the opposite side.

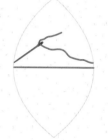

Step 3

Continue working the bars to the top of the shape and then work the lower section in the same way.

TIP

If you want to add patterns once you have worked the grid, decide on the pattern first because this will determine the size of the squares you need.

Step 4

You can now start working the vertical bars. Start the vertical bars in the middle of the shape. It is important to stitch the bars at 90 degrees to the bars already worked so that you create squares.

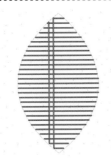

Step 5

Work the vertical bars in the same way that you worked the horizontal ones, until the shape is covered.

Step 6

Once you have worked the grid, you need to secure the bars. At the moment, the stitches are very long and it would be easy to catch them. Work small diagonal stitches where the threads cross. Keep these stitches small so that they do not encroach too much into the squares. Take care to ensure that the squares are not distorted by pulling on the bars.

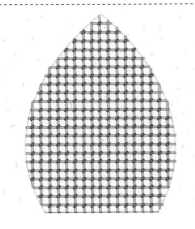

TIP

If you are not sure where to bring up the needle, poke the needle halfway through the fabric and lay it down on the fabric. This gives a good guide to where the stitch will lie without you actually working a stitch.

CHAIN STITCH AND DETACHED CHAIN STITCH
━━ TUTORIAL ━━

Chain stitch is a continuous line of interlocking loops, each held down by the next one. You can work chain stitch in a single line or as a series of rows to fill an area. A single chain stitch on its own is known as a detached chain stitch or lazy daisy stitch.

Materials
- Fabric (any)
- Embroidery or chenille needle
- Thread
- Embroidery scissors

CHAIN STITCH

Step 1

Bring the needle up and down within the same hole, 1. Before pulling the needle down, ensure that a loop is left on the top of the fabric. With the loop still visible, bring the needle up along the design line, at the length that you wish the stitch to be, 2.

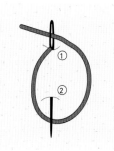

Step 2

While holding the needle in the loop, with the other hand gently pull down the thread that remains underneath the fabric. Bring the needle and thread all the way up through the loop, 2. You are now ready to start the second stitch.

Step 3

Take the needle back down to 2, then bring it up a stitch distance below to 3. Continue in the same way along the design line.

Step 4

To end the row, instead of taking the needle back down within the loop, insert it just below to 4, to work a small securing stitch.

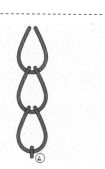

DETACHED CHAIN STITCH

Step 1

Work a single chain stitch as described in Step 1 of chain stitch (up and down at 1, back up at 2, and down at 3), but finish the loop as in Step 4 of chain stitch.

Step 2

You can work four or five detached chain stitches in a circle to make a flower.

STEM STITCH
TUTORIAL

Stem stitch is a popular outline stitch. When worked with the loop to the opposite side, it is called outline stitch.

Materials
- Fabric (any)
- Embroidery or chenille needle
- Thread
- Embroidery scissors

Step 1

Bring the needle up at the start of the design line, 1, and take the needle down further along to 2. Pull the needle and thread through the fabric, leaving a loop of thread on the top of the fabric. Keep the loop to the right and bring the needle up in the middle of the stitch along the design line to 3. Pull the needle and thread up. You have completed the first stitch, and this is where you start the next one.

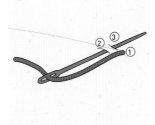

Step 2

Take the needle down further along the design line to 4, keeping the loop to the right. Try to keep the stitches the same length. Bring the needle up halfway along the stitch; this should be where the last stitch ended, 5.

Step 3

Continue along the design line, working the stitches in the same way. Every time you work a stitch, keep the loop to the same side. When working upward, it is easy to remember that the loop is always to the right.

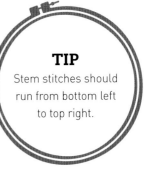

TIP
Stem stitches should run from bottom left to top right.

LONG AND SHORT STITCH

—— TUTORIAL ——

Long and short is a very popular stitch and is the stitch used in silk shading. It is very dense and suitable for most areas. With silk shading, long and short stitch should create an area with graduated shading, so use a number of shades from one color range.

Materials
- Fabric (any)
- Embroidery needle for each shade of thread
- Threads in a range of shades
- Embroidery scissors

Step 1

You need to work a split stitch around the shape first (see steps 1–2, page 184). This ensures that you will achieve a neat, crisp edge. Use one strand in your needle.

Step 2

Long and short stitch is worked in rows across a shape. The stitches should vary in length, with some of them long and some of them short. (It is best to think of it as long and longer, since really short stitches will limit where you can bring up the stitches in the second row.)

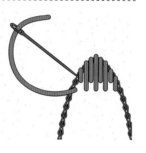

Step 3

The second row is worked slightly differently; you bring the needle up in the previous row of stitches and take it down into the design shape. Continue to vary the length of the stitches and where you bring the needle up.

Step 4

New shades should be introduced gradually, so try working two needles at the same time. When working more than one needle, pick which needle to use. When not working the other color, "park" the needle within the design area, so that it is out of the way. The following row should be worked in the same way, by splitting the stitches and working down the design.

TIP
When you are at an edge and need to cover the split stitch, work the stitch from inside the design and take it down over the split stitch line.

BLOCK SHADING
—●— TUTORIAL —●—

Block shading is a dense stitch suitable for most areas. It is worked in rows so lends itself to using a range of colors within a design.

Materials
- Fabric (any)
- Embroidery or chenille needle
- Threads
- Embroidery scissors
- Ruler

Step 1

Work a split stitch (see steps 1–2, page 184) around the top edge of the design, so that you create a crisp edge.

Step 2

Draw on the different colored bands you would like to work, making sure they are even in size—a ruler may help to keep them even. Starting in the middle of the design line, to ensure you work at the correct angle, bring the needle up and work the stitches as for satin stitch (see page 184), but vertically. Tuck the needle over the edge of the split stitch.

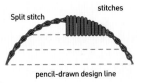

Step 3

Keep the stitches as close together as possible so that no fabric is visible. For the second row, bring the needle up from the bottom (on the next design line) and take the needle down into the edge of the first row of stitches, splitting the threads.

Step 4

Work the next row in the same way, working the stitches from the bottom (on the next design line) and taking the needle down into the second row of stitches, splitting the threads.

CORAL STITCH
— TUTORIAL —

Coral stitch is a decorative outline stitch that looks like a straight line with evenly spaced knots along it. Coral stitch is most effective when worked with two or more threads in the needle.

Materials
- Fabric (any)
- Embroidery or chenille needle
- Threads
- Embroidery scissors

Step 1

Starting at 1, bring the needle up and lay the thread along the design line, the way you will travel. Holding the thread, take the needle down through the fabric above the thread, 2. Pull the thread down halfway, so you have a loop on top of the fabric. Bring the needle back up through the fabric beneath the thread and inside the loop, 3.

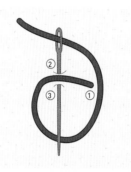

Step 2

Hold on to the needle and gently pull the thread to draw up the loop and create a knot. You have now completed the first stitch. Continue along the design line, trying to keep the knots evenly spaced.

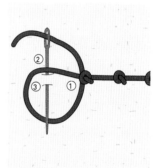

Step 3

If you are working more than one row of coral stitch, you can "brick" the knots to give the effect shown here. To do this, work the knots of the second row so that they lie between the knots of the first row.

TIP

For a neat finish, make sure the knots you create are evenly spaced, especially when working a number of rows side by side.

FRENCH KNOT STITCH
— TUTORIAL —

French knots are small, round stitches. To achieve larger knots, use more threads in your needle. You can use a combination of colors in the needle to create larger, variegated knots.

Materials
- Fabric (any)
- Embroidery or chenille needle
- Thread
- Embroidery scissors

Step 1

Bring up the needle at 1 and wrap the thread around the needle once.

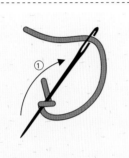

Step 2

Take the needle back down at 2, close to where it came up, keeping hold of the thread that is still wrapped around the needle. Slide the thread down the needle so that it is touching the fabric.

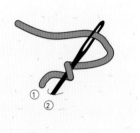

Step 3

Keeping the remaining thread taut, pass the needle through the fabric, leaving the knot on the surface. Take care not to pull it too tightly or the knot may disappear to the back of the fabric.

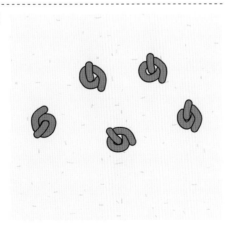

TIP
The most difficult part of making a French knot is achieving the correct tension. Keep hold of the thread until the needle is about to pass through the fabric.

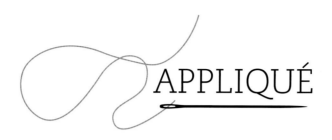

APPLIQUÉ

Appliqué comes from the French word *appliquer*, meaning to "put or lay on." It involves attaching a cut-out decoration on a larger piece of fabric. The most successful pieces of appliqué combine the placement of different fabrics along with surface stitching to create beautifully simple but effective designs.

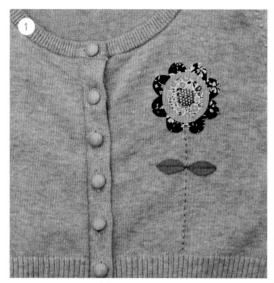

1. Appliqué flower worked using cotton and felt on a knitted background with surface stitching worked in stranded cotton *by Kirsty Neale*.
2. Appliqué of a peacock worked in a range of fabrics, including cotton, velvet, and organza, using cottons, silks, and cords *by Sarah Homfray*.

3. Appliqué worked on printed cotton, stitched in embroidery floss *by Corinne McHie*.
4. Three-dimensional appliqué hydrangea created with cottons, stitched with embroidery floss *by Corinne McHie*.

Appliqué has a long history—the earliest-known example is a canopy of leather decorated with symbolic serpents and blossoms, dated 980 B.C., which can be found in the Boulak Museum in Cairo, Egypt. It is believed that the idea of appliqué was first discovered when clothes ripped and they were mended by artistically sewing a different piece of material over the top of the rip. There is historical evidence of the use of appliqué in many cultures of the world. A variety of materials have been used in appliqué designs, including beads, fish scales, and tree bark, which have been stitched on a huge variety of stitchable surfaces.

From the 15th century, appliqué began to replace crewelwork on household linens, probably for the purpose of extending the life of these textiles or as an imitation of time-consuming "raised" embroidery. Appliqué was used on the banners and cloaks of the Christian Crusaders (11th to 16th centuries). The Elizabethans (1558–1603) used the appliqué technique by itself and in conjunction with quilting to decorate clothes, quilts, curtains, wall hangings, and cushions. They often used fine leathers.

To this day, appliqué has been used as a heavy embellishment by the Church for religious garments, wall hangings, and altar cloths. Modern uses of appliqué extend throughout the home furnishings range of cushion covers, bedspreads, pillowcases, and curtains. With the help of the modern sewing machine appliqué can be worked onto many items of clothing and accessories to transform otherwise ordinary items into works of art. The technique of appliqué allows embroiderers to create an interesting surface in a relatively short amount of time.

New products—including a range of products that stop cut fabrics from fraying, and fibers that temporarily fuse fabrics together—have turned appliqué into a versatile technique.

4

TIP
Satin stitch, stem stitch, and coral stitch can all be worked along the edge of an applied fabric.

Surface Embroidery

STAB STITCHING
— TUTORIAL —

Stab stitching consists of very small stitches generally worked to secure an applied fabric to a base fabric. Once the fabric is secure, you can decide which decorative stitch to work around the shape. This depends on the design you are using.

Materials
- Pins
- Fabric (any)
- Embroidery needle
- Sewing thread
- Embroidery scissors

Step 1

Pin the applied fabric shape in place on the base fabric.

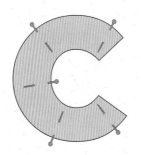

Step 2

Bring the needle up from the base fabric and down into the applied fabric shape.

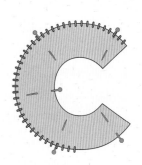

Step 3

These stitches can be left visible or you can work a decorative stitch over them.

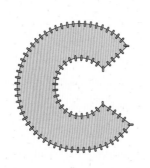

TIP
With large shapes, work a few stab stitches to keep the applied fabric in place, then go back and work stitches every couple of millimeters.

COUCHING 1

— TUTORIAL —

Couching is laying down threads along the design or applied fabric edge and working small securing stitches over it. The thread lying on the fabric should be the correct thickness to cover the raw edge. The color can be matched to the applied fabric to blend in, or to a complementary color so that it becomes a design feature.

Materials

- Fabric (any)
- Couching thread
- Securing thread, finer than the couching thread
- Embroidery needle
- Chenille needle
- Embroidery scissors

Step 1

Lay the couching thread on the design. Using the embroidery needle, thread up the securing thread. Make sure you leave a tail at the start of the shape that can be plunged to the back of the fabric to finish it off. Sew small, evenly spaced stitches over the thread.

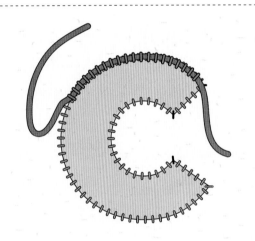

Step 2

Once you have worked around the shape, use the chenille needle to plunge both of the couching-thread ends to the back of the fabric and work a couching stitch over the join. Then sew over the ends on the back to secure them.

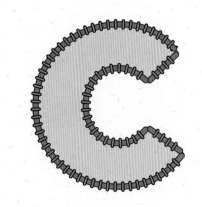

TURNING UNDER
— TUTORIAL —

Instead of stab stitching the shape down (see page 36) and working a decorative stitch over the stab stitches, you can turn the edges under so that the applied fabric has no stitches visible. This is a fairly difficult technique to master.

Materials
- Fabric (any)
- Fabric scissors
- Pins
- Curved or embroidery needle
- Sewing thread
- Embroidery scissors

Step 1

Cut out the applied fabric so that it is larger than it needs to be by about ¼ in/6 mm, then fold this edge under all the way around the shape. If you have a shape with curves, make cuts into the edge every so often to help the fabric lie flat when folded under the edge. Pin this piece of fabric onto the background, folding the excess under as you go.

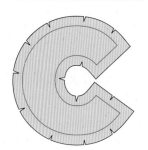

Step 2

Using a strand of sewing thread and a needle (a curved needle may make this process easier), bring the thread up on the base fabric on the design line and run a stitch along the fold of the fabric. The stitch should be invisible because it is in the fold.

Step 3

Take the needle and thread out of the applied fabric and down into the base fabric. Bring the needle up further along the background fabric and again work a stitch along the fold of the fabric. This stitch is called a slip or ladder stitch. If worked correctly, there should be no stitches or thread visible.

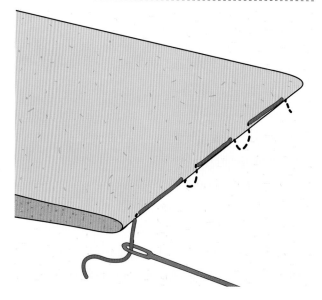

APPLYING A CORD

— TUTORIAL —

You can make a cord that either matches or contrasts with the fabric to which it is applied. See the Cord tutorial (page 224) for how to make a cord. The cord is applied so that it sits on top of the stab stitches and applied fabric.

Materials
- Fabric (any)
- Cord and matching sewing thread
- Embroidery needle
- Embroidery scissors
- Chenille needle

Step 1

Attach the applied fabric to the background fabric using a small stab stitch (see page 36) all the way around the shape. The cord will be placed on top of this, so ensure the stitches are small and will be covered. Lay the cord on the shape, leaving a tail, which can be taken to the back and finished off later.

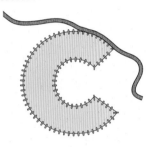

Step 2

Bring up a thread that matches the color of the cord and work stitches into the cord. Work the stitches so that they fall into the gap in the cord. It is important to work the stitches in the same direction as the twist of the cord.

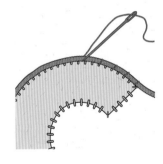

Step 3

Continue to work the stitches around the design. When you get back to the start, you can plunge both ends of the cord to the back. (Thread them into a chenille needle and take them to the back; you can then oversew them onto the back of the piece.) Try to make the join as neat as possible; you may need additional stitches here to hide the join.

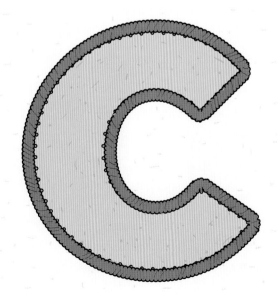

SILK SHADING

Silk shading is a beautiful, delicate technique that creates
subtle shading and realistic effects. It is often used
in conjunction with other techniques such as goldwork;
the gold threads beautifully complement the flat areas
of color produced by silk shading. Since silk shading
is a very time-consuming technique, it is usually
used for small items such as cushions
and framed fabric pictures.

The production of silk started in China over 4,000 years ago, and early Chinese garments were elaborately embroidered with rows of shaded chain stitch. Silk shading is also known as long and short stitch. In England, from the 11th to the 14th centuries, many professional embroideries were produced for the abbeys and monasteries. These were large pieces of solid embroidery, and the hair and draperies of the religious figures depicted in them were often worked in rows of silk shading. After the dissolution of the monasteries by Henry VIII in the 1530s, the production of embroidery for the Church came to an end for a while.

However, outside of the Church, silk shading was popular in Britain during the Tudor period (1485–1603). Owing to the increase in trade with the Far East, a wide range of richly colored silks were used for magnificent dress embroideries and for the furnishings of the large houses that were built at the time. A variety of items were made; the designs were mostly of flowers, animals, and birds. For the home there were cushions, quilts, fire screens, and wall hangings. Clothing included skirts, jackets, waistcoats, gloves, shoes, hats, and purses. During this period, stumpwork embroidery (see page 136) was becoming popular, and silk shading was often found on the flat areas of boxes and mirror frames.

During the 18th century, embroidered classical figures became popular, and the method of silk shading gave the work a painted look known as needle painting. The designs were often taken from classical figurative engravings; silk shading was ideal for creating a painted effect. Embroiderers produced elaborate pieces of silk shading worked onto fabric and sold them to dressmakers and tailors to be used on clothing.

The basic technique of silk shading has not changed, although the subjects now worked are a little more varied. The threads and colors available have increased because of industrial development. The wider choice of colors means that silk shadings can be even more realistic than in the past. Silk shading is mostly worked in stranded cottons because these are readily available at a modest price, although some embroiderers still use silks.

TIP

It is best to work from a high-resolution photograph so that your shading is as realistic as possible.

Surface Embroidery

SILK SHADING PRIMER

Planning

The best silk shadings are worked from real life so that the embroidery is as accurate as possible. Therefore a photograph is the best design source to use. Once you have the photograph, you then need to match the colors to stranded cottons. Pick out all of the colors that you see in the image. If you are struggling to see the different colors, pull out one strand of the stranded cotton and lay it on the part of the photo where you think it could be used. You work embroidery in one strand so this is the best way to see the color as it will appear. The stranded cottons come in six strands, which create a much stronger color.

The order of work in silk shading is very important. Once you have an image, take a couple of photocopies so that you can determine which elements will be in the foreground and which will be in the background. Always work the background parts first.

Threads

In silk shading, you can thread up all the possible shades so that you can pick them up and use them as required. Anywhere between 10 and 20 needles may be used at the same time. When you are not using a thread, bring up the needle within the design lines and leave it on top.

When you have picked out all of the threads, lay them out in their different color groups, for example, so that all of the reds are together. Write down the number and make of all the threads, from darkest to lightest. This will help you pick a color when working on each area.

Note that colors such as red and yellow are quite hard to work with because the range of threads available is limited. If it helps, use a range of different brand cottons to achieve the full color range.

Outlines

First of all, you work a split stitch to outline the shape (see steps 1–2, page 184). You need to keep the split stitch as small as possible and worked to a good tension, to ensure that the edges are neat.

Stitches

For silk shading, you use one strand of cotton or silk and work in long and short stitch (see page 30). It is important to start and finish the threads within design lines since these will be completely covered with the silk shading. There should be no gaps in the embroidery—each stitch should be worked side by side. Then as you work within an area, you split the stitches of the previous row to work the next row. This means that a large part of the stitches worked in the previous row will be covered by the next row. This is quite a hard concept to understand; it is unlike any other stitch.

When working silk shading, it is important to regularly stand back from your work to check how effective it is. Often stitching that looks wrong close up is in fact extremely effective at a distance—which is generally how the piece will be viewed when completed.

NATURAL SILK SHADING
———— TUTORIAL ————

In natural silk shading, the stitches are worked following the direction of the subject, so the stitches curve with the design. Natural shading is used on flowers, fruit, and natural objects where there is a growth line and direction. The colors of the stitches should blend into one another.

Materials
- Fabric (any)
- Pencil
- Embroidery needle
- Threads in a range of colors
- Embroidery scissors

Step 1

It is important to follow the direction of each part of the design. For a flower, you need to plan the petals and leaves. Make a photocopy of your flower. Work out the different shades, directions, and order of work. Mark the outlines and stitch directions onto your fabric in pencil. Work the background areas first, then toward the front of the flower.

Step 2

Work a split stitch, in a medium shade, to outline the first area you will work (see steps 1–2, page 184). Use long and short stitches (see page 30), to cover the split-stitch edge. This stitch should produce curves, so the rows should flow into one another with no abrupt angle changes.

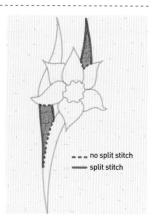

- - - no split stitch
——— split stitch

Step 3

When working areas that sit on top of one another, make sure you work a small, neat split stitch that slightly overlaps the top of the previous area. This is so that when you work the silk shading, you can tuck the needle around the split-stitch edge and no fabric will show. It should look like one area is worked on top of the other, which is realistic.

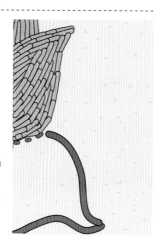

TIP
Remember that most of the stitches you work will be covered by the next row of stitches. The length of the stitch will partly depend on the area that you are working in. In a small area, the stitches can be slightly shorter. Wherever possible, work long and short stitch, but for very small areas, you may require satin stitch (see page 184).

Step 4

Consider the shades used on every area: each needs to look different from the one next to it, especially at the edges. However, the colors in a photograph sometimes need to be slightly tweaked in stitch. If two edges of a petal look very similar, it is best to change them a little, so that the petals as well as the split-stitch edge are defined with color. Note that petals that are underneath others will have a slight shadow, created by the petal on top.

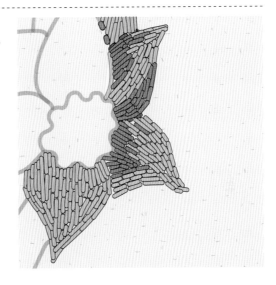

Step 5

If the middle of the flower is textured, it is best to work it in other surface stitches, such as French knots (see page 33). These stitches add to the three-dimensional effect created by the silk shading.

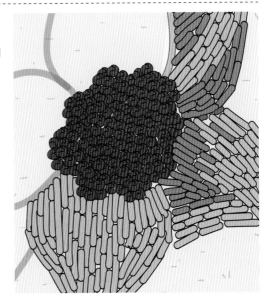

TIP

Work by the light of a daylight bulb to ensure you are creating the most realistic embroidery you can. This is especially useful on dark winter days.

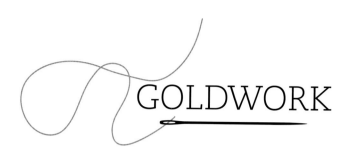

GOLDWORK

Goldwork involves sewing metal threads onto fabric.
The threads are not placed in the needle but are
usually couched down. Although the technique
is mostly referred to as goldwork, the threads come
in gold, silver, and copper. It is a fairly delicate
technique, which takes practice to perfect.

For 2,000 years, goldwork has been a symbol of opulence and distinction. It is thought to have originated in China; silk merchants brought the craft to Europe. The first metallic threads were of pure gold, which was beaten and cut into strips and then wound around a silk core and used for couching.

The earliest surviving example of English goldwork embroidery is the St. Cuthbert maniple from the 10th century; the gold fibers were added to the surface of the fabric rather than woven into it. Throughout the Middle Ages and the Renaissance period (5th to the 17th centuries), goldwork grew in popularity for opulent costumes and furnishings for the Church, royalty, and aristocracy in Europe. During the Elizabethan period (1558–1603), gold and metallic embroideries, including pearls and precious stones, were used lavishly to decorate clothing worn at English and continental courts.

By the early 17th century, embroidery techniques had changed and the technology for producing fine gold threads had advanced. Fine gold and silver threads were often combined with blackwork (see page 94) and silk embroidery; the gold threads were stitched into coiling stem patterns to link a pattern of flowers or birds.

In the early 19th century, goldwork had lost its popularity and was limited to use in haute couture, although it remained important for military, religious, and ceremonial textiles—and is still used on ceremonial church vestments today.

The introduction of cheaper substitutes has increased interest in goldwork techniques. The range of "metal threads" available has expanded; threads can be bought in gilt or 2 percent gold, silver, and copper, and a wide range of colored purls can be found. Goldwork is still considered a precious embroidery technique, mostly used on framed pieces of embroidery; the nature of goldwork restricts its use. It is often highly padded and therefore vulnerable to damage, and it cannot be washed, which makes it difficult to use on clothing. However, goldwork is used in fashion accessories around the world and is widely used to decorate Indian saris—which can be dry cleaned. With the threads now readily available and affordable, goldwork has become a popular embroidery technique once again.

TIP
Store metal threads in acid-free bags to ensure they do not tarnish.

APPLYING FELT PADDING
— TUTORIAL —

When you apply felt padding, use layers of felt in a color that matches your threads, so that if there are any gaps, the visible padding is less obvious. For gold threads, use yellow felt; for silver, use gray; and for copper, use orange. Felt padding is used for most goldwork because it is fairly easy to apply and can be built up to a reasonable level.

Materials
- Fabric scissors
- Felt in a color to match metal thread
- Fabric (any)
- Pins
- Sewing thread in suitable color
- Embroidery needle
- Embroidery scissors

Step 1

With fabric scissors, cut out the layers of felt. The amount of felt required depends on the design; you cannot apply a lot of layers to very small shapes. The largest piece should be slightly smaller than the design shape, so that once applied it sits just inside the design line. Cut out each layer of felt so that it is slightly smaller than the last one.

Step 2

Apply the layers of felt from the smallest up to the largest so that the top layer is smooth and creates a good surface for the metal threadwork. Place the first piece of felt in the middle of the shape and pin it to the background fabric.

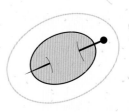

Step 3

Using one strand of sewing thread that matches your metal and felt, bring the needle up in the background fabric and down in the felt, working a stab stitch (see page 36). Continue working around the shape. To keep the felt in the correct place, work once around the shape, leaving large gaps, and then go back around, ensuring stitches are worked with gaps of approximately ⅛ in/3 mm.

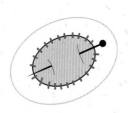

Step 4

Apply subsequent layers of felt in the same way.

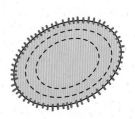

APPLYING STRING PADDING

— TUTORIAL —

You can use string padding when you require more padding in a narrow band. This is typical of cutwork, which requires thin bands of highly padded areas.

Materials
- Fabric (any)
- Soft cotton string
- Wax
- Sewing thread
- Embroidery needle
- Embroidery scissors

Step 1

Wax a long length of soft string. This makes the string easier to manage. Fold the string in half, and half again, until you achieve the correct width for the design shape: about 2 in/5 cm longer than the shape. The height of the string is up to you—as long as the string sits just within the width of the shape.

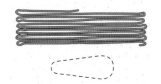

Step 2

Thread up a double sewing thread. Starting with the widest part of the band, work a couching stitch (see page 37) across the string.

Step 3

Continue to work couching stitches across the string evenly along the band. Where the shape becomes narrower, remove some of the string. The neatest way to remove it is to lift up the string and remove pieces by cutting the string from underneath; then the top layer remains smooth.

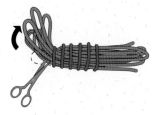

Step 4

Once you reach the end, work some securing stitches into the end of the band, coming up at the end and down into the string. These stitches hold the string and neaten the edge.

COUCHING 2

TUTORIAL

Couching—laying down a core thread and working holding stitches over it—is a main stitch used in goldwork. It is an unobtrusive way of securing metal threads because the couching stitches won't stand out. The stitches should be worked at a 90-degree angle to the couched thread.

Materials
- Fabric (any)
- Metal thread
- Sewing thread
- Embroidery needle
- Chenille needle
- Metal thread scissors
- Curved needle

Step 1

Sew metal threads in pairs. Leave a 2 in/5 cm tail. Bring a single strand of sewing thread up on the design line and down the other side of the metal thread. Do not stitch so tightly that the metal threads are pushed on top of each other.

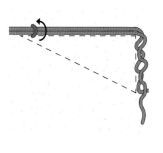

Step 2

Work evenly spaced stitches along the design line. If you need to turn a corner, work up to it, then couch the two metal threads separately. Bring the needle up on the outer thread and couch into the center of the pair. Do the same with the inner thread.

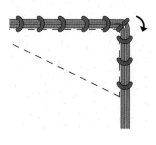

Step 3

Work the second row of couching stitches in between the first, bricking the stitches. Angle the needle to the first row so that no fabric shows in between the rows. (Space is shown in this diagram so that the "bricking" of stitches can be seen.)

Step 4

At the end of the shape or design line, secure all threads at the back of the piece. Thread a single metal thread into a chenille needle and take the needle down to the back of the fabric. Do the same with the sewing thread.

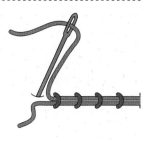

Step 5

Turn over the embroidery. Using a curved needle and sewing thread, oversew the metal thread into the back of the couching stitches. Take care not to catch into the fabric; this will create a stitch in the front of the piece too.

WORKING WITH PEARL PURL
— TUTORIAL —

Pearl purl is a stiff metal coil that you couch into the grooves. When you are starting and finishing, you simply cut the thread.

Materials
- Fabric (any)
- Pearl purl
- Waxed sewing thread
- Embroidery needle
- Tweezers
- Embroidery scissors
- Metal thread scissors

Step 1

Stretch the pearl purl slightly. This allows the sewing thread to fall in between the grooves of the thread, which will make the stitches invisible. Lay the pearl purl onto the design and bring up a single strand of waxed sewing thread. Work a small couching stitch in the direction of the grooves.

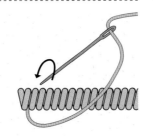

Step 2

Work stitches every couple of grooves so that the pearl purl is secure.

Step 3

To turn a corner, use tweezers to pinch the thread. Cut the pearl purl when you get to the end of the design line.

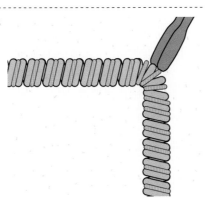

TIP
If a metal thread unravels when cut, you should couch it and plunge the ends to the back of the piece.

CHIPPING
— TUTORIAL —

Chipping is worked over felt padding. The process involves cutting small, square beadlike pieces of bright-check purl, which are then sewn down in random directions to fill a shape. A pearl-purl outline must be worked first to outline the shape and give you a structure to fill with the chips.

Materials
- Fabric (any)
- Waxed sewing thread
- Pearl purl
- Metal thread scissors
- Bright-check or wire-check purl
- Beading mat or velvet board
- Sewing thread in suitable color
- Embroidery needle

Step 1

Using the beading mat, cut a pile of purl chips before you start; ideally they should be square. Wax a double strand of sewing thread and thread this through the needle.

Step 2

Outline your shape with pearl purl. Bring the needle up at the edge of the shape, close to this outline, and pierce a chip with the needle. Take the needle down about ⅛ in/3 mm along so that the chip sits on the felt padding.

Step 3

Bring the needle up close to the last chip and thread on the next one; this can then be taken down close to the previous chip. Work the chips in random directions.

Step 4

Fill in the whole area keeping the chips random and not in straight lines, ensuring that no felt remains visible. The chips should all lie on the felt with no sewing thread visible.

TIP
Keep a separate pair of embroidery scissors for cutting metal threads because they will blunt scissors.

USING KID LEATHER

— TUTORIAL —

Kid leather comes in a range of colors and is often used in goldwork. If you can, buy leather that is intended for embroidery, since it will be soft and easy to stitch with. Padding underneath kid leather works really well but make sure, if you use it, that the leather is tight to avoid wrinkles.

Materials
- Fabric (any)
- Kid leather
- Template
- Pencil
- Paper scissors
- Embroidery needle
- Sewing thread in suitable color

Step 1

Use a template and trace it to get the shape you want on the back of the leather. Cut out the shape.

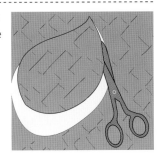

Step 2

Place the leather on the design on the background fabric. For large shapes, baste first to hold in place.

Step 3

With sewing thread, bring the needle up in the background and work small stab stitches (see page 36) all around the kid leather, keeping the stitch length consistent and the stitches evenly spaced.

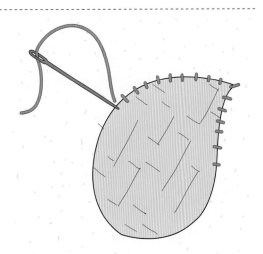

TIP

Make sure that the stitches are not too small because they will rip the leather.

CUTWORK

━━━━ TUTORIAL ━━━━

Cutwork is one of the most difficult techniques to master and one of the most delicate. It is always worked over an area padded with soft string (see page 49) and should be one of the last parts of a design to be worked, to avoid damaging it. When transporting cutwork, create a window using bubble wrap to protect it.

Materials
- Fabric (any)
- Purls: smooth purl, rough purl, bright check, or wire check
- Beading mat or velvet board
- Soft string
- Metal thread scissors
- Wax
- Sewing thread
- Embroidery needle

Step 1

Using the beading mat, cut a length of purl sufficient to cover the area padded with soft string. Always cut two purls the same size so that you can use the second one as a guide. Wax a double strand of sewing thread and bring the needle up to the middle of the soft string.

Step 2

Place the purl onto the needle and over the soft string. If you are happy with the length, push the purl down the thread and check again that it is the right size. If not, trim the purl or cut a longer one. When working up the soft string, the needle comes up on the right and goes down on the left. Take the needle down at 45 degrees, so that it is sitting bottom left to top right, just outside the soft string. Bring the needle up again with a long stitch on the back to work the next purl.

TIP
You can work the purls in any combination. Bright and wire check are easier to work with as they are more durable. Smooth and rough purls are harder to work with since they are easily damaged.

Step 3

Continue working the purls upward over the string. No padding should show between purls so ensure that they are close together. If the shape tapers off or gets wider, adjust the template purl accordingly.

Step 4

Once you reach the end of the soft string, go back to the middle and work downward, following the same method. This time you are coming up on the left and going down on the right.

Step 5

Continue until the shape is completely covered.

TIP

Take care to cut the purls to the correct length. If they are too long, they will be loose, which could cause the purl to crack; if they are too short, the sewing thread and soft string will be visible at the ends.

MARGARET DIER

PROFILE

Margaret's work is inspired by nature. Architecture is another passion of hers, especially weather-beaten buildings. She finds Venice inspiring for her embroidery because the colors are amazing. Margaret usually paints a watercolor picture and then embroiders from that. She also carries her digital camera everywhere so she can capture images that inspire her. Then she does a small sketch that becomes her working drawing. She prefers not to plan the embroideries too much; letting the piece evolve is far more satisfying.

"Often I draw the design straight onto the fabric with a pencil without any sketch at all. I am too impatient and want to get stitching."

Margaret generally mixes different techniques in each piece. She likes to use appliqué with surface stitching because it adds great interest to the textures of the embroidery. She uses traditional stitches but in a contemporary way. For example, when she stitches silk-shading embroidery, she likes to cut out the embroidery after working it flat in a frame; this totally transforms the original piece. The time Margaret spends on each piece varies greatly. A small sketchy type piece takes one or two hours, while a larger piece can take anywhere from 75 hours or more!

In terms of materials, Margaret uses a lot of silk fabrics, which give a sense of luxury to her work. She also loves bold printed fabrics; just a small amount can bring a contemporary feel to her piece. For threads, she likes to mix many different types. Space-dyed threads (threads dyed in a repeated sequence of colors) are great to use—you have no control over the color mix so they produce unexpected results. However, the main threads she uses are stranded cottons. They are cheap and come in every color you could possibly need.

1. Natural silk-shaded cat worked in stranded cottons on a silk background fabric.
2. Natural silk shading of a butterfly worked on a painted background.
3. Appliquéd cotton shapes and surface stitches worked on a silk background; stitches worked in a black machine thread.
4. Three-dimensional silk-shaded pansy with a wired edge, made into a brooch.

> "Always have a ring frame with a scrap bit of fabric in it for trying out ideas, and don't throw it away—it is a visual record of what works and what doesn't."

Margaret usually exhibits her work at small textile fairs, where she enjoys the opportunity to talk to people about her embroidery. They are always fascinated to learn how her pieces are stitched and constructed. She encourages people to have a go themselves and teaches workshops.

Specialty
Surface embroidery, especially silk shading

Inspired by
Old book covers

Experiments with
Mixing techniques in one embroidery

Most challenging project
Capturing pets' personalities with long and short stitch

Top tip
Always have a ring frame ready to try things out on.

Shop
Works to commission

CHAPTER 2

COUNTED SURFACE EMBROIDERY

Counted surface embroidery describes any embroidery
for which you are required to count the threads of the
fabric to work a series of stitches. It often involves
working a repeating pattern. In order for the stitches
to create successful patterns, they must
all be worked to the same size and, for this,
an evenweave fabric is required.

1. Canvas work in tent stitch using tapestry wools on canvas *by Liz Smith*.
2. Cross stitch worked in stranded cottons on Aida *by Kimberly Scola*.

Counted Surface Embroidery

1. Bargello cushion worked in tapestry wools on 12 tpi canvas *by Margaret Burns* (photo by Alison Poole).
2. Canvas-work cushion worked in tapestry wool on 10 tpi double canvas *by Harihi Okubo.*
3. Canvas coasters worked with tapestry wools on 10 tpi double canvas *by Harihi Okubo.*

4. Golden bee worked in cross stitch in metallic threads on 24-count fabric *by Sophie Simpson*.

5. Blackwork fish worked in silk threads on linen *by Mary Corbet*.

Counted Surface Embroidery

1. Portrait of Maureen Barter in blackwork worked on linen *by Lucy Barter*.
2. Cross-stitch silhouette worked in stranded cotton on linen *by Sophie Simpson*.
3. Black cross-stitch horse worked in stranded cottons on 32-count natural linen *by Tina Fitzpatrick*.

4. Canvas-work kit worked in
silk and ivory threads on canvas
by Heather Gray.
5. Canvas shading worked in
crewel wools on 18 tpi canvas
by Sophie Long.

1. Canvas-work cushion with tent stitch and cushion stitch worked in tapestry wool on canvas *by Liz Smith.*

2. Cross stitch worked in stranded cottons on Aida *by Samantha Purdy.*

3. Cotton sewing thread worked on cereal
in cross stitch *by Judith Klausner*.
4. Mabel the pug worked in blackwork on linen
by Sophie Long.
5. Cross-stitch heart buttons worked in
stranded cottons on Aida *by Samantha Purdy*.

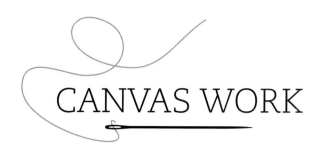

CANVAS WORK

Canvas work, often referred to as "tapestry" or "needlepoint," is a popular transition step from basic cross stitch to more creative hand-embroidery techniques. This counted-thread technique is worked on a canvas that comes in a range of sizes. Evenweave fabric is measured in threads per inch (tpi). For example, 18 tpi means that there are 18 threads in an inch of that canvas. The larger the count, the more stitches can be worked in a square inch.

1. Canvas work using embroidery floss and crewel wool *by Abigail Timmis.*
2. Canvas-work knot garden, worked in a range of threads *by Owen Davies.*
3. Canvas-work floral design worked on 18 tpi canvas *by Grace Walsh.*
4. Canvas work using cotton floss, wool, and metallic threads *by Laura Mason.*

Canvas work is the name given to embroidery that is worked on a canvas grid. It is also known as needlepoint or tapestry because tent stitch resembles the look of a tapestry, which is woven on a loom. Embroidering onto an evenweave material similar to canvas dates back to Roman times. A range of tribal groups used geometric counted-thread textiles to make carpets and furnishings.

When stumpwork (see page 136) became popular during the Elizabethan period (1558–1603), "slips" were often worked on canvas. A slip is a small piece of canvas that is stitched, and then the shape is cut out and applied to another fabric; during the Elizabethan period, the fabric would often have been velvet. In the late 16th century, canvas work was also used to create beautiful purses.

The 17th century saw canvas-work pieces used for pictorial embroideries rather than household items. The basic stitches were Gros point and Demi point.

In the first part of the 18th century, canvas work grew in popularity, and chairs were commonly upholstered with canvas-work embroidery. Canvases were often painted by artists and then passed on to professional embroiderers to be completed for the customer.

In the 19th century Berlin work (typically wool worked in cross stitch on canvas) made canvas work even more popular. The subjects were often sentimental, such as pets and bouquets of roses. These pictures were originally worked completely in cross and tent stitch with worsted wools; later, embellishments such as beads and jewels were added.

Canvas work saw a decline in the first part of the 20th century. Since Berlin wool work was normally worked from patterns, people often felt it lacked originality. Fine canvas work enjoyed a comeback when it was reintroduced for making church furnishings, especially kneelers, owing to its hardwearing qualities.

Canvas work today offers many opportunities. A huge range of threads are available, allowing embroiderers to experiment with creating modern pieces of art. Since it is hardwearing and suitable for home furnishings, canvas work continues to be used for cushions and wall hangings.

SLANTED GOBELIN STITCH
— TUTORIAL —

This is a small slanted stitch that is worked in rows. You can work this stitch horizontally or vertically, depending on the design. You can also work it at different scales, depending on the canvas size and the area you are covering.

Materials
- Canvas
- Tapestry needle
- Threads
- Embroidery scissors

Step 1

Start this stitch at the top right of the design area. Bring the tapestry needle up at 1 and take it down at 2.

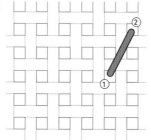

Step 2

Bring the needle back up at the bottom at 3 and take it up to 4. Continue working these stitches along the row.

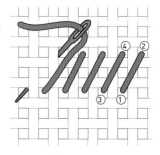

Step 3

Work the second row from left to right, again working the stitches from the bottom diagonally upward from 5 to 6 and then down to 7.

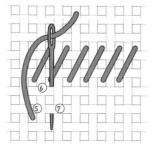

Step 4

Continue to work these rows.

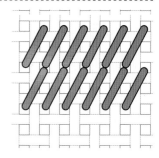

TIP
The stitch can be made slightly longer by going over one more square in the canvas. This will allow you to work fewer stitches within the design area and cover the canvas quicker.

MOSAIC STITCH
─ TUTORIAL ─

This is a small square made up of three diagonal stitches. It is a small stitch that you can use in small- to medium-sized areas to work fairly complex shading and create a textured background.

Materials
- Canvas
- Tapestry needle
- Threads
- Embroidery scissors

Step 1

Working from the top right of the canvas, bring the needle up at 1 and down at 2. Then bring the needle up at 3, which is the hole next to 1, and take the needle down above 2 to 4. To complete the square, bring the needle up at 5 (which is above 3) and take it down at 6 (which is next to 4). The square is complete.

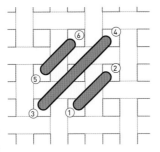

Step 2

Continue working squares along the row. The next row is worked in the same way; all of the small stitches sit in a diagonal row, as do the long stitches.

Step 3

These squares can be worked in one color or in different colors, depending on the design.

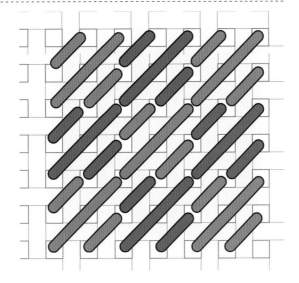

MILANESE STITCH
━○━ TUTORIAL ━━

This is a diagonal pattern made up of triangles that have four stitches in each. The Milanese stitch is fairly big, so work it in large areas to show the pattern clearly. It can be shaded or worked in rows of different colors to achieve stripes.

Materials
- Canvas
- Tapestry needle
- Threads
- Embroidery scissors

Step 1

Start this stitch at the top left of the canvas. Bring the needle up at 1 and down at 2, working a small stitch. Then bring the needle up at 3 (which is below 1), and down at 4 (which is next to 2). Bring the needle up at 5 and down at 6, then back up at 7 and down at 8. The triangle is complete.

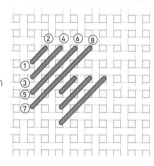

Step 2

Bring the needle up below the last stitch in the middle to start the next triangle. Work the next triangle below the first.

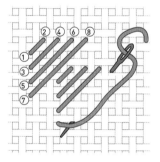

Step 3

The second row is worked from the bottom right to the top left, fitting the triangles next to each other. This row is worked so that the triangles are the other way up. There should be no gaps between the triangles.

TIP
You can work a stripy stitch if you alternate the colors used in the diagonal rows.

HUNGARIAN DIAMOND STITCH

— TUTORIAL —

This is a small diamond stitch that is worked in rows. You can work this stitch horizontally or vertically, depending on the design. You can also work it at different scales, depending on the canvas size and the area you are covering.

Materials
- Canvas
- Tapestry needle
- Threads
- Embroidery scissors

Step 1

Starting at the top right of the canvas, bring the needle up at 1 and work a straight stitch down at 2. Bring the needle up at 3 and down at 4, and bring the needle up at 5 and down at 6. Bring the needle up at 7 and down at 8, then up at 9 and down at 10. This completes one diamond.

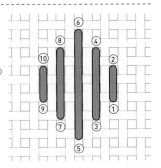

Step 2

Leave a gap of one hole, then start the next diamond. Continue working across the design, leaving one hole between each diamond.

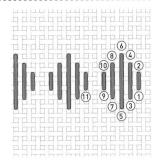

Step 3

Work the second row in the same way. The diamonds in the second row are linked to the diamonds in the first row. The empty hole left in the first row is filled by the longest vertical stitch in the middle of each diamond.

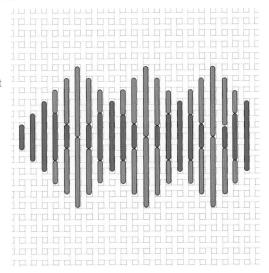

TIP
Leave a gap between each row of diamonds to allow for the points of the next row.

DOUBLE CROSS STITCH

— TUTORIAL —

This is a stitch made up of a large cross and then four smaller crosses worked on each side. It is a fairly big stitch and therefore needs to be worked in large areas, where you wish to create texture. The small and large crosses can be worked in the same color or different colors, depending on the design.

Materials
- Canvas
- Tapestry needle
- Threads
- Embroidery scissors

Step 1

Start at the top right of the canvas. Bring the needle up at 1 and down at 2, four threads to the left and four threads down. Come up at 3 and down at 4, to create a cross. Work a row of large stitches from right to left, starting your next cross at 3.

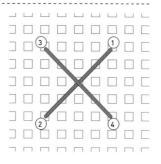

Step 2

To work the smaller crosses, bring the needle up at 5, above the bottom tip of a diamond, work a straight stitch up to 6, then bring the needle up at 7 and down at 8. Complete the row in this way.

Step 3

Work the next row with small crosses only, this time from left to right.

Step 4

Now work another row from right to left, as in steps 1–2. Continue to work large and small crosses in this way to fill out your design.

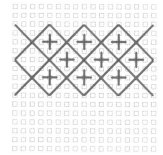

TIP
Work the top threads of the crosses in the same direction. Try working the diamonds in different colors to create a tile-pattern surface.

STAR STITCH

— TUTORIAL —

This stitch is worked in rows to create raised star shapes. It is a textured stitch that is suitable for medium to large areas.

Materials
- Canvas
- Tapestry needle
- Threads
- Embroidery scissors

Step 1

Start near the top left of the canvas. Bring the needle up at 1 and work a straight stitch to 2. Then bring the needle up at 3 and down at 4. This creates a cross. Then bring the needle up at 5 and down at 6. To complete the second cross, bring the needle up at 7 and down at 8.

Step 2

Work a second star in the same way, to the right of the first star. The arms of the stars should share the same hole.

Step 3

For the second row, work the top of the star into the same hole that the arms of the previous row used. Ensure that you work the stitches in the same order so that the thread that is lying on top always goes in the same direction.

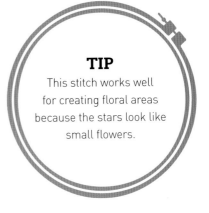

TIP

This stitch works well for creating floral areas because the stars look like small flowers.

RICE STITCH

— TUTORIAL —

This is a cross stitch that is made up of a large stitch with the corners crossed. Rice stitch creates a relatively raised texture because you work the additional stitches only over the corners. Work rice stitch in large areas; you can work it in one color or work the smaller stitches in the corners in a different color.

Materials
- Canvas
- Tapestry needle
- Threads
- Embroidery scissors

Step 1

Start this stitch at the top right of your canvas. Bring the needle up at 1 and down at 2, then up at 3 and down at 4 to create a cross.

Step 2

Work a diagonal stitch across one arm of the cross by bringing the needle up at 5 and down at 6. Repeat this for each arm.

Step 3

Work another large cross. The arms of the first cross should share the holes of the second cross so that no canvas is visible. Repeat the diagonal stitches on each arm.

Step 4

Work the subsequent rows in the same way. To work in two colors, work all of the large crosses first and then use the second color to do the diagonal stitches on each arm.

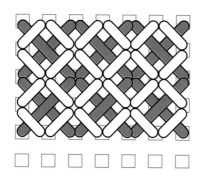

TIP
Try shading the stitches by changing the colors of the large crosses.

CIRCULAR EYELET STITCH
— TUTORIAL —

This is a stitch made up of 16 stitches to create a daisy-like eyelet. You can work it in large areas to create floral patterns.

Materials
- Canvas
- Tapestry needle
- Threads
- Embroidery scissors

Step 1

Start this stitch at the right of the canvas. Bring the needle up at 1 and down at 2 (this will be the middle of the flower). Then bring the needle up at 3 and back down at 2.

Step 2

Continue to work the stitches, always going down into 2. This becomes more difficult as you work more and more stitches into 2. When you have made 16 stitches, the eyelet is complete.

Step 3

Bring the needle up at 10 to start the next eyelet.

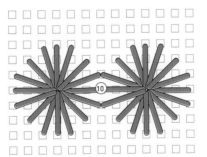

Step 4

In the second row, the eyelets fit in between the ones in the previous row, sharing the holes in the canvas.

TIP
If you are struggling to pass through at 2, try using fewer threads in the needle. This will also prevent damage to the canvas.

CANVAS SHADING

Canvas shading is canvas work that is worked in one stitch, typically tent stitch. The details of the design are worked in different colors and shades of threads. Canvas shading is most effective when worked from an original source, such as a photograph. This allows the embroiderer to create realistic shading, often making new shades by mixing threads in the needle.

1

Like canvas work, canvas shading is worked on canvas but generally only one stitch is worked: tent stitch. This small stitch allows you to work detailed designs that are shaded. Throughout history, this type of embroidery has often been worked in silk or wool, with the occasional use of metal threads for embellishment.

Tent stitch first appeared in the 13th century when it was combined with stitches that were worked in a range of directions on one piece of canvas. Later on, petit point was introduced for canvas work used for home furnishings; this was suitable for cushions and seat coverings because it was flat and hard wearing. Canvas work has been used for a variety of decorative items, including bed and wall hangings, church kneelers, and seat cushions.

Tent stitch was used to create stunning table carpets, often worked onto canvas that was 20 tpi (threads per inch); one of the earliest examples was made about 1550. Embroidered canvas table covers were extremely popular in Holland. The size of the canvas and of the finished piece—often over 10 ft/3 m long—made them a focal point of the room.

Canvas shading was also used to create purses in the late 16th century. It had another valuable purpose: young girls worked canvas as an embroidery training piece.

Today, stunning pieces of canvas shading are worked in a range of threads, including wools, stranded cottons, and silks, with finished embroideries made into dramatic pieces of art or homewares, such as cushions.

(2)

TIP

When you choose your colors, test to see if they will blend together by working a small square of the colors next to one another. This is especially useful when you are blending colors in a needle.

TENT STITCH

⟶ TUTORIAL ⟵

Tent stitch is the most basic canvas stitch. It is a small diagonal stitch, worked over one thread of the canvas. It allows even small areas to be worked in detailed shading. The size of the tent stitch depends on the count of canvas used. There are a number of ways of working tent stitch; when working the main design, where lots of colors are used, it is best to work in horizontal rows across the canvas.

Materials
- Canvas
- Tapestry needle
- Threads
- Embroidery scissors

Step 1

Working from right to left, bring the needle up at 1 and down at 2, up again at 3 and down at 4. Continue in this pattern across the line.
To check whether you are working it correctly, look at the back of the canvas. You should have a long diagonal stitch worked all the way across the row.

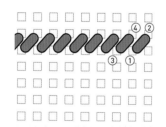

Step 2

For the next row, work from left to right. Bring the needle up at 5 and down at 6 and then up at 7 and down at 8. Continue across the row.

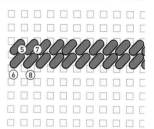

Step 3

Work the next row from right to left. Continue this pattern for the whole design.

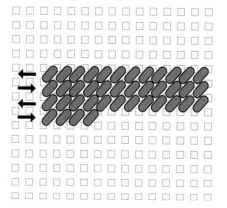

TIP

Where multiple needles are used, work the stitches in rows. Avoid jumping around the canvas because this creates bulk on the back where the threads cross over.

BLENDING IN THE NEEDLE
━ TUTORIAL ━

To broaden the range of colors in canvas work, you can mix two colors of a similar tone in the needle to create a new shade. Using multiple needles with different combinations allows you to create smooth and subtle color changes.

Materials
- Canvas
- Tapestry needle for each color combination
- Wools in range of colors
- Embroidery scissors

Step 1

Thread up the different color combinations. You can use different types of thread, for example, stranded cottons and wool. Do samples of color combinations before working on your piece and take note of which colors blend successfully. It helps to leave a knot next to the sample piece to identify the thread combination.

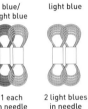

blue   blue/light blue   light blue

2 blues in needle   1 each in needle   2 light blues in needle

Step 2

Work tent stitch (see facing page), bringing up your correct color combination in each place.

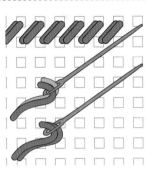

Step 3

Mix the colors gradually, slowly increasing the number of stitches that are worked in the new combination and decreasing the use of the other colors. For strong color changes, you work fewer rows blending the combinations.

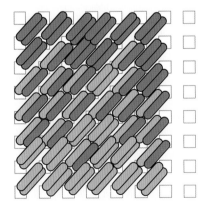

TIP
When a needle and thread are not in use, bring them to the top of the canvas, within a design line that will be worked in a similar color. Do not bring the needle up in the background; the thread may leave fluff that will be visible when you work the background in a different color.

BASKETWEAVE STITCH
— TUTORIAL —

Once the main design is complete, you can then stitch the background. Basketweave stitch is worked in diagonal rows and is ideal for working a background in one color.

Materials
- Canvas
- Tapestry needle
- Threads
- Embroidery scissors

Step 1

Bring the needle up at 1 and work a stitch to 2. Then leave a gap and bring the needle up at 3 and down at 4. Continue in the same way to the end of the row.

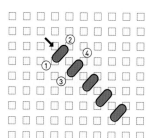

Step 2

In the second row, you work the stitches in the gaps between the stitches in the previous row, coming up at 5 and going down at 6. If you are working the background to fit into a square, the rows will gradually get longer until you reach the middle of the square, from where they will become smaller as you work along the bottom of the square.

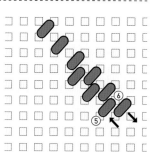

TIP
Working tent stitch in horizontal rows often results in a slightly stripy appearance; this is not a problem when you are working areas that are shaded. However, if you are working the background in one color, it is best to use basketweave tent stitch because it is worked in diagonal rows.

STRETCHING THE CANVAS
— TUTORIAL —

When working canvas, it is very important to work it in a frame, so that the tension is consistent. However, once the canvas is removed from the frame, it may lose its square shape. If you intend to mount the canvas or make it into a cushion, use this method to restore its shape.

Materials
- Old sheeting
- Wooden board
- Hammer
- Tacks
- Embroidered canvas piece
- Set square
- Bowl of cold water
- Cloth

Step 1

Put some old sheeting over the wooden board to prevent the wood from marking the canvas. Use the hammer to knock in tacks all the way around the canvas, in the area outside the design. Use the set square to pull the canvas straight and square as you go. It may be helpful to use one or more of the edges of the wood to help you to maintain a straight line. Pull the canvas as tight as you can.

Step 2

Using the cloth, gently dampen the canvas by dabbing it with water. Do not rub it; this will damage the stitches and they will become matted or fluffy. Make sure all the canvas is damp—the stitching and the excess canvas. This will wash out some of the stiffener, so you can manipulate it more.

Step 3

Go back around the board, pulling the canvas out to straighten it. Keep checking it with the set square. Once it is as square as possible, leave the canvas to dry. If you are not satisfied with the result when it is dry, you can repeat the process.

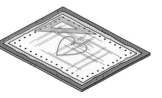

TIP
Draw your design with a permanent ink pen and ensure that all of your threads are colorfast before you stretch the canvas.

BARGELLO

Bargello needlework uses a range of colored threads, traditionally wools, to create repeated geometric designs. The embroiderer has to count the threads of the canvas and work a series of straight stitches in shaded threads to create three-dimensional effects. All of the stitches used in Bargello are flat, vertical stitches.

Bargello, also known as Byzantine work, is a form of canvas or needlepoint. Its origins lie in the upholstery of a set of 17th-century chairs found in the Bargello Museum in Florence, Italy, which feature a "flame stitch" pattern. At that time, it was a popular technique in the tiny workshops, convents, and colleges in Florence and Bargello was handed down from generation to generation.

Bargello embroidery is distinguished by its use of straight, vertical stitches, the most basic of which are Gobelin, Brick, and Hungarian. With these stitch types and colorful woolen threads, Bargello has been used for hundreds of years to create stunning designs on rugs, cushions, shoes, chair covers, and upholstery.

In the 1970s Bargello became hugely popular for furniture coverings throughout the Western world. In recent years, it has gained popularity with updated designs that include the use of different types of thread. Traditionally, Bargello was stitched on a canvas background but recent designs use any openweave fabrics (such as linen) to create a similar effect.

Although the technique has remained the same, modern uses of Bargello-style embroidery can be found on cushions, jewelry, belts, chair covers, and wall hangings. Embroiderers can purchase a variety of interesting pre-printed canvases to stitch from the Internet or craft shops. Many books are also available, and owing to the revival of this unique style, modern designers have expanded the repertoire of design options. It is also possible for embroiderers to invent their own designs by working a series of straight stitches in a range of patterns.

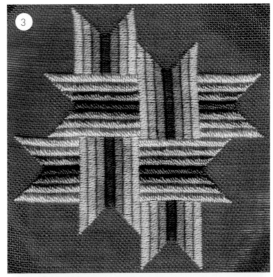

ZIGZAG STITCH

— TUTORIAL —

Zigzag stitch is made up of single stitches worked over four threads of the canvas in steps of one (see Tip below). It has a relatively small repeat so you can use it in small areas of a design or for narrow bands.

Materials
- Canvas
- Threads in five shades of one color
- Tapestry needles
- Embroidery scissors

Step 1

Start this stitch in the middle of the canvas and work the first row from right to left in the lightest shade.

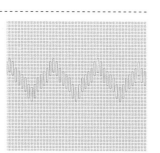

Step 2

Work the second row in the next shade from left to right, above the first row, using the first row to help with your placement.

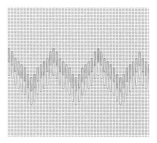

Step 3

Continue to work the next three rows in the same way, each time using a shade darker than the one before. Once you have worked five rows, return to the lightest shade and repeat the process.

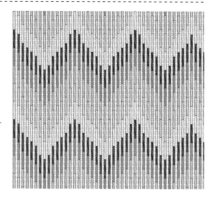

TIP
To create the staggering of stitches in Bargello, each stitch needs to be worked higher or lower than the previous stitch. "Steps of two" means to work each stitch two canvas threads above or below the previous stitch; "steps of one" means one thread above or below.

ZIGZAG STITCH

PATTERN

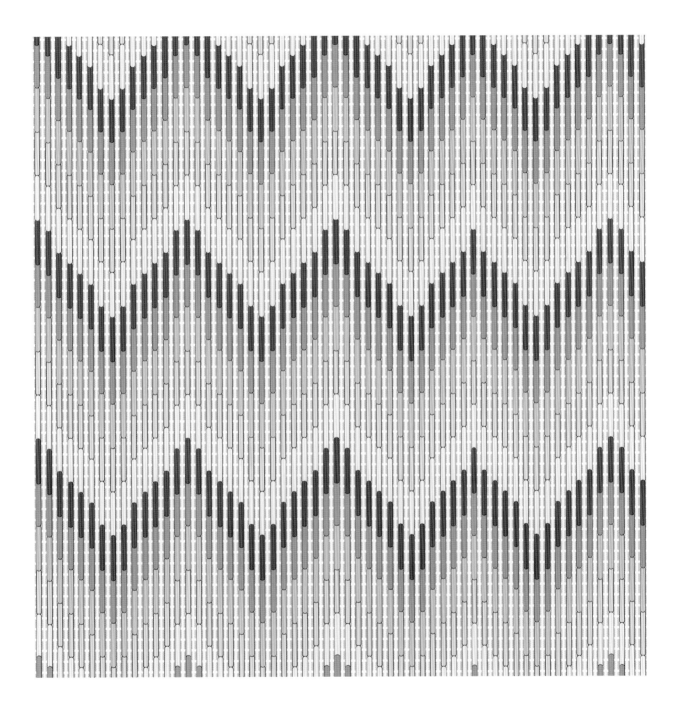

HEART STITCH
━ TUTORIAL ━

Heart stitch has stitches over four threads in steps of two (see Tip on page 84), from single stitches to groups of four. It is best to work this stitch over a relatively large area because the repeat is quite large. You need to work a couple of repeats of the pattern to be able to see it clearly.

Materials
- Canvas
- Threads in five shades of one color (for hearts) and two shades of a contrasting color (for diamonds)
- Tapestry needles
- Embroidery scissors

Step 1

Start this stitch at the base of one of the hearts with the lightest of the five heart shades. Fill your design area with heart outlines, working upward from left to right or right to left as required.

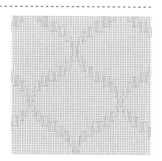

Step 2

Fill in the heart shapes, working the shades from the lightest at the bottom to darkest at the top row of the heart.

Step 3

Work the diamond above the heart, starting with the lightest shade at the top of the heart and working the darker shade above that.

Step 4

Continue to work this pattern, working the hearts and then filling in with the diamonds.

TIP
Try reversing the colors, using the darkest shade at the bottom of the hearts.

HEART STITCH

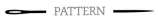 PATTERN

RIPPLE STITCH
— TUTORIAL —

Ripple stitch has stitches over four threads in steps of two (see Tip on page 84), in blocks of one to four. Although this stitch has a small repeat, you need to work it in a fairly large area, ideally in a diagonal band, so that you can see the direction of the ripples.

Materials
- Canvas
- Threads in six shades of one color
- Tapestry needles
- Embroidery scissors

Step 1

Work the first row from the top right to the bottom left. Start the first row in the lightest color.

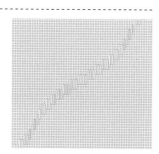

Step 2

Work the second row in the next shade from top right to bottom left, above the first row.

Step 3

Continue to work the remaining four rows, each time using a darker shade until you have worked all six of the shades. Start the pattern again with the lightest shade and work through, again using a darker shade each time until you reach the darkest. Repeat until your design area has been filled.

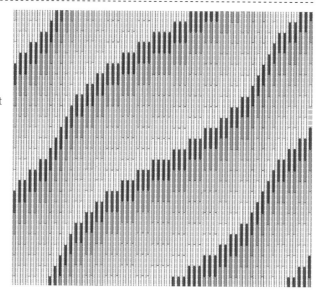

RIPPLE STITCH

 PATTERN

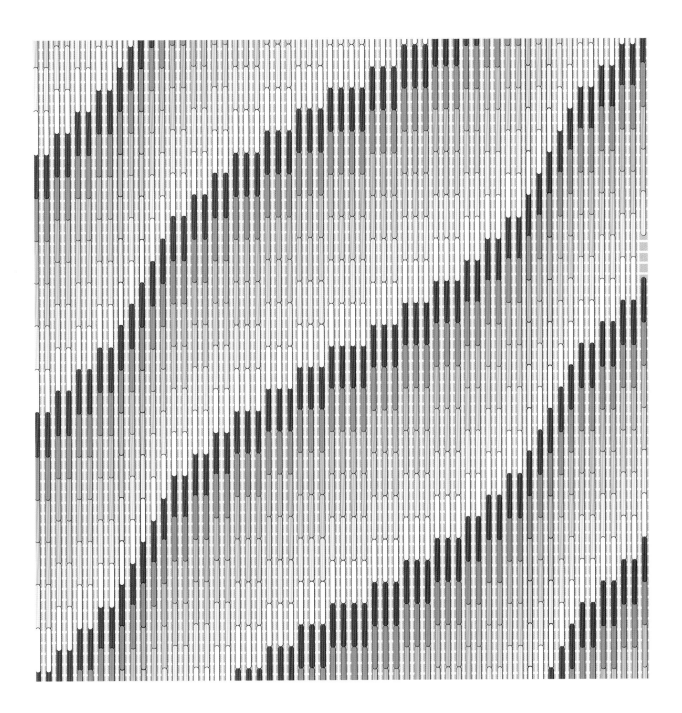

NORTHERN LIGHTS STITCH
— TUTORIAL —

Northern Lights stitch has single stitches worked over four threads in steps of two (see Tip on page 84). This is a relatively small repeat so it can be worked in a small area. You can also work the pattern vertically, depending on the design.

Materials
- Canvas
- Threads in four shades of two colors
- Tapestry needles
- Embroidery scissors

Step 1

Work the first row with the lightest shade of one of the colors. Start in the middle, work out to one side and then return to the middle and work out to the other side.

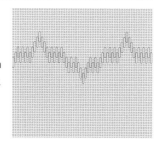

Step 2

Work the next row below this in a darker shade. Continue to do this until you have worked all four shades.

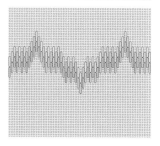

Step 3

Work the following row in the lightest shade of the second color. Work all four rows in this new color, going from the lightest to the darkest shade.

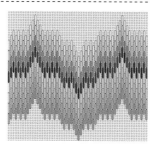

Step 4

Continue to work rows of all four shades, from light to dark, in each of the two colors until your design area has been filled.

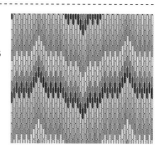

TIP

For smaller areas of canvas, use fewer shades; for larger areas, you could add more shades.

NORTHERN LIGHTS STITCH

PATTERN

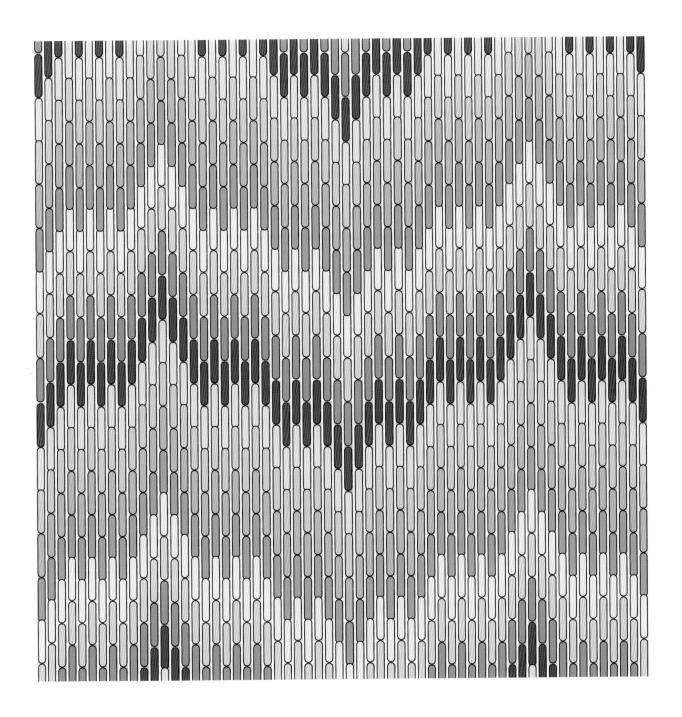

JACOBEAN SPIRES

— TUTORIAL —

This is the most complex of the patterns; make sure that you count each stitch carefully. It makes a really stunning pattern but does require a large area to see its full effect. The stitch consists of single stitches over six threads and single stitches over two threads in steps of one (see Tip on page 84).

Materials
- Canvas
- Threads in three shades of one color and six shades of another color
- Tapestry needles
- Embroidery scissors

Step 1

Follow the pattern on the facing page. Start in the center of your design area. Work the first row in the lightest of your three-shade color.

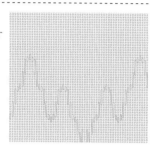

Step 2

Work a second row above this with the middle shade of your three-shade color, and a third above that in the darkest. Repeat this below your first row, with your middle shade below your light, then your darkest.

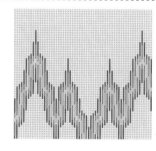

Step 3

Now take the darkest of your six-shade color and return to the top of your design. Work through your shades as before, but from darkest to lightest and back to darkest.

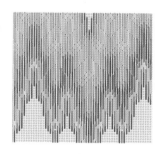

Step 4

Still with your six-shade color, return to the bottom of your design and repeat. Continue to work the rows in this way, referring to the pattern on the facing page.

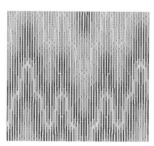

TIP

Generally, two long stitches are followed by two short, but at the peak you may need to work three short or three long stitches.

JACOBEAN SPIRES

PATTERN

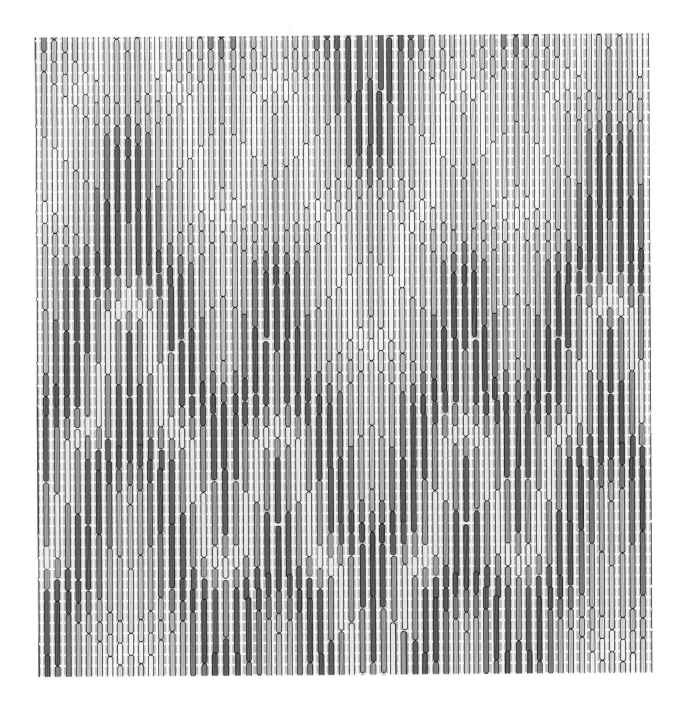

BLACKWORK

Blackwork is mostly worked in black thread but is
sometimes worked in red, green, and blue. The name
blackwork refers more to the stitches and patterns
worked than to the color. Blackwork is a counted-
thread technique that is used to create patterns for
samplers, or the stitches can be shaded to create
three-dimensional embroideries, for example,
of people or buildings.

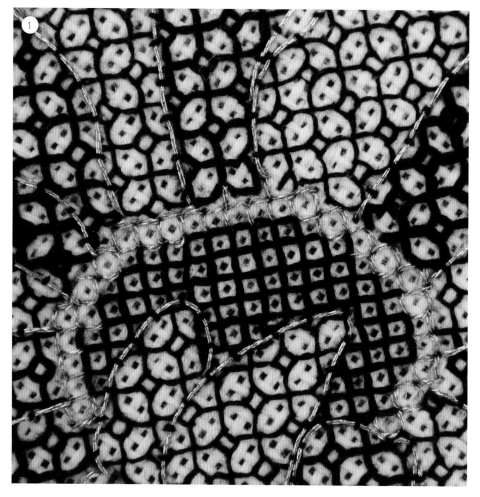

1. Close-up of blackwork flower worked in stranded cottons and metallic gold thread *by Sophie Long.*
2. Blackwork portrait of Coral Long, worked in a range of black threads on linen *by Sophie Long.*
3. Blackwork worked on linen in silk, stranded cotton, and coton á broder *by Terri King.*

It is believed that blackwork originated in Spain and was brought to England by Catherine of Aragon, the first wife of Henry VIII. Blackwork became popular during Henry VIII's reign (1509–1547); repeat counted patterns were worked to form simple decorations on collars, cuffs, and household linens.

Early examples of blackwork used only straight stitches in the patterns, with no diagonal or slanting stitches. When a stitch was worked, it either followed the warp or weft threads. The straight stitches made the patterns quite jagged. Later on, diagonal stitches were added to soften patterns and shapes.

By the time of Elizabeth I (1558–1603), blackwork embroidery had become more complex and was used to cover large areas of fabric with intricate patterns. The early 17th century saw a decline in the popularity of the technique. It reappeared by the 19th century but was mainly restricted to use on household linens.

The 1920s and 1930s saw a revival of blackwork, and by the late 20th century designers were using the varying tones of the different stitches to build their designs. Embroiderers can now use blackwork to create realistic images of buildings and portraits by using the different thickness of threads to create light and dark areas. Sometimes color is added to these pieces.

TIP
Create shading by varying the thickness of the threads you use.

BLACKWORK PRIMER

PLANNING

When choosing which stitches to use, consider the kind of image you are re-creating. For example, if you are working a face, keep the stitches simple and circular, but if you are working a plant, you can use more intricate and floral stitches.

If you would like to play with some stitch ideas, use a piece of graph paper for sketching them out. Any pattern is possible as long as you work stitches using the holes of the linen.

If you are leaving areas that are highlights in the design with minimal or no stitching, be aware that any threads you pass behind these areas, on the back of the design, may be visible when you mount it.

THREADS

The threads most often used for blackwork, from thinnest to thickest, are:

- gossamer silk thread
- machine embroidery thread
- stranded cotton
- coton á broder

Ophir thread, though less common, can be used to add a silver or gold highlight.

OUTLINES

Shapes should be defined using the stitches you are working to shade your design. If the design is dark and well defined, it is best not to include any outlines. The most successful blackwork

pieces are those without outlines. If the shape of a particular area is left unworked because it is light, you can work a simple stem stitch (see page 29), but outline stitches should be kept to a minimum.

If you do need to work an outline, make sure you change to an embroidery needle; this will allow you to pierce the threads of the fabric to create smooth curves, so you will not be restricted to the holes of the fabric. Use chain stitch (see page 28) for thicker outlines. It can be worked in any of the threads to achieve different thicknesses. For fine outlines, use the finer threads and work in stem stitch because it creates a delicate line.

STITCHES

There are thousands of blackwork patterns and very few rules about which stitches should be used for this technique. The scale and size of the stitch will depend on the count of the linen you use: with finer counts, in which there are more threads per inch, the stitches will be smaller, which allows you to achieve more intricate shading. The order you work a stitch does not really matter—as long as you are counting the threads correctly, you will end up with the same result.

SQUARE STITCH
━ TUTORIAL ━

This is the smallest stitch that can be worked; it is very useful for small areas, such as eyes on people or animals.

Materials
- Evenweave fabric
- Tapestry needle
- Black thread
- Embroidery scissors

Step 1

Bring up the needle and work a stitch that goes over one thread of the fabric vertically. Then come up one thread across from this and work a stitch back into the same hole. You now have half of a box.

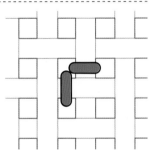

Step 2

Work the other two sides of the box; each stitch shares a hole of the fabric with another stitch.

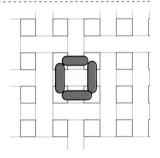

Step 3

Once you have worked one box, continue working from there outward so that all of the boxes are touching.

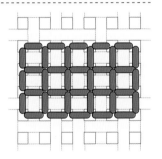

Step 4

To make the stitch darker for dark areas of the pattern, you can work a diagonal stitch across the box. When worked in thick thread, this will create a filled-in box.

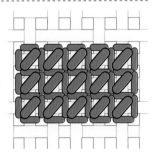

TIP
The most effective pieces of blackwork are often ones where there are areas without stitches that create a highlight or contrast between dense areas of stitches.

SMALL DIAMOND STITCH
— TUTORIAL —

This stitch is slightly bigger than the square stitch on the previous page. It is made up of diagonal shapes that each have a vertical straight stitch in the middle.

Materials
- Evenweave fabric
- Tapestry needle
- Embroidery scissors
- Threads

Step 1

Bring up the needle in a hole and work a diagonal stitch. Go two threads up and then two threads across and down into that hole.

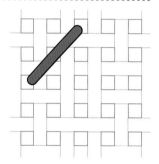

Step 2

Bring up the needle in the hole that is two threads below that and two threads to the right. Work a stitch back into the last stitch. You have worked half of the diamond.

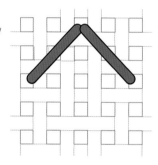

Step 3

Work the other half of the diamond in the same way. Then work a stitch from the middle of the diamond to the peak.

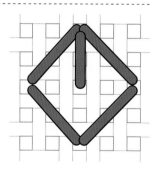

Step 4

Continue to work the diamonds so that they are all touching. To add shading to this stitch, you can work a cross in the middle of the diamonds.

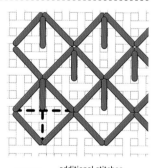

- - - - - additional stitches to add shading

HONEYCOMB 1
━━● TUTORIAL ●━━

This pattern is made up of hexagonal honeycomb shapes with a box in the middle. It is useful for large areas and its curves make it suitable for natural objects.

Materials
- Evenweave fabric
- Tapestry needle
- Embroidery scissors
- Thread

Step 1

Bring the needle up and work a vertical stitch over two threads of the fabric. Then bring the needle up two threads horizontally across from that stitch and take the needle back down into the first stitch's hole.

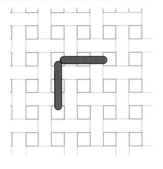

Step 2

Work the other two sides in the same way to complete a box. Bring the needle up one thread across from the first stitch and work a parallel line. Do the same on the other side of the box.

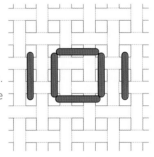

Step 3

Bring the needle up at the end of the vertical stitch and take it back down two threads horizontally and two threads above it. Work in the same way to create the second point. Do the same on the other side of the shape to create points at both ends.

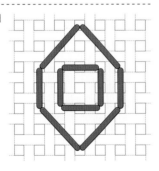

Step 4

Work the honeycomb shapes in rows so that they are all touching. To add shading to this stitch, you can work a diagonal stitch or a full cross within the boxes.

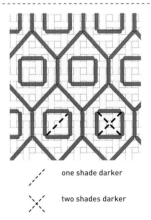

╱ one shade darker

╳ two shades darker

TIP

In blackwork, it does not matter how the stitches are worked; work them in a way that is convenient for you.

OPEN HONEYCOMB
—— TUTORIAL ——

This is similar to the honeycomb stitch on page 99. It consists of a condensed hexagon with a vertical stitch in the middle. Open honeycomb is a fairly open stitch so it is not suitable for areas that you require to be really dark.

Materials
- Evenweave fabric
- Tapestry needle
- Embroidery scissors
- Threads

Step 1

Bring the needle up at 1 and work a vertical stitch over two threads of the fabric. Then bring the needle up two threads above and two threads to the right, at 3. Work a stitch from here to the last stitch, at 4.

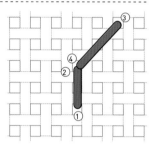

Step 2

Bring the needle up where the second stitch started, at 5, and work a horizontal stitch over two threads of the fabric, taking the needle down at 6. Bring the needle up two threads below and two threads to the left, at 7, and work a stitch back to the start of the last stitch, at 8. Create a horizontal stitch to complete a small stretched diamond, bringing the needle up at 9 and down at 10. You have worked a quarter of the stitch.

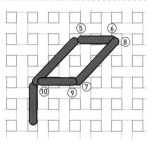

Step 3

Work a stretched diamond in the three remaining corners of the shape. On the sides, there is a vertical stitch to join them; you have already worked this on the left side.

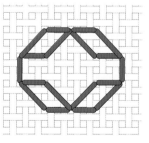

Step 4

Work a vertical stitch in the middle of the shape over two threads of the fabric. You can make the stitch lighter by not working this stitch. Leaving out stitches is a useful technique for adding shading by creating lighter areas within your design.

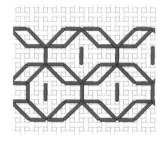

OCTAGONAL SQUARE

— TUTORIAL —

This stitch consists of crosses and squares worked in rows. It is fairly small and is useful for natural shapes, such as faces, because it is quite circular.

Materials
- Evenweave fabric
- Tapestry needle
- Embroidery scissors
- Thread

Step 1

Bring the needle up and work a cross over two threads of the fabric.

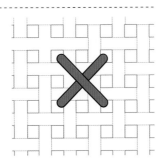

Step 2

Bring the needle up at the end of the cross and work a vertical stitch over two threads of the fabric. This is one side of the box. Work the other three sides of the box, each stitch working over two threads of the fabric. Then work a cross at the top-right side of box. Repeat the process, working a box and then another cross.

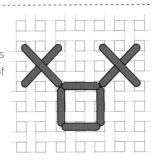

Step 3

Repeat the pattern on the row below. Each cross that is worked has a box attached to each of the arms and each box that is worked has a cross attached to each corner. To make this stitch darker, you can work a diagonal stitch across the central squares.

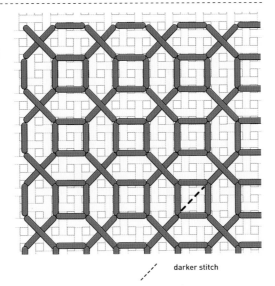

darker stitch

FLORAL LACE
— TUTORIAL —

This large, pretty stitch is very effective for foliage and natural shapes. It consists of four basic honeycomb shapes with a large cross worked in the middle. It is quite large so it is best worked in big areas where the pattern is clear.

Materials
- Evenweave fabric
- Tapestry needle
- Embroidery scissors
- Thread

Step 1

Bring the needle up and work a vertical stitch over two threads of the fabric. Bring the needle up two threads to the right and two threads above. Work a stitch back into the end of the first stitch.

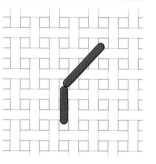

Step 2

Go to the bottom of the first stitch and work a stitch two threads below and two threads to the right. This is half of the honeycomb stitch. Work the mirror image on the other side. Then you work another honeycomb shape, at a 90-degree angle to the first.

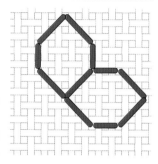

Step 3

Work two more honeycombs, rotating at 90 degrees each time. The fourth honeycomb should meet up with the first. Then work a straight stitch inside each honeycomb, from the middle of each comb to the center of the flower, over three threads of the fabric.

Step 4

The honeycomb group is then repeated, so the peak of one honeycomb group forms the middle of the next one. You create the small boxes by working the honeycombs. It is not possible to make this stitch much darker since it is fairly open.

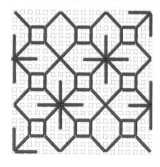

TIP
First, try out stitches on the fabric you will be using—the number of threads per inch will affect how dark the stitches are.

LACE
TUTORIAL

This fairly difficult stitch is very decorative. It is suitable for covering large areas, creating a floral pattern. It is made up of floral shapes and long diamonds. Lace stitch is fairly light when worked since it is quite open.

Materials
- Evenweave fabric
- Tapestry needle
- Embroidery scissors
- Thread

Step 1

Bring the needle up and work a diagonal stitch over two threads of the fabric. Then work another three diagonal stitches, all going down into the middle to create a cross.

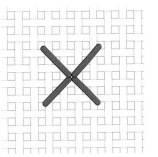

Step 2

Create honeycomb shapes from each arm of the cross by working a series of vertical, diagonal, and horizontal stitches as shown, each over two threads of the fabric. Work four honeycomb shapes around the cross.

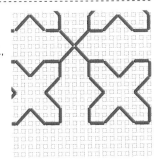

Step 3

Work a cross in the center of each group of four honeycombs. Each stitch is worked over two threads of the fabric.

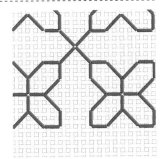

Step 4

Work a cross as in Step 1 from the points of the honeycombs.

Step 5

In each space between two honeycombs, work a diamond with straight stitches over two threads. At the top and bottom of each diamond point, work a straight stitch over two threads to finish.

CROSS STITCH

Cross stitch is based on two stitches that form a cross, and is a counted-stitch technique carried out on a canvas or evenweave fabric. It is based on regular shapes and so produces schematic rather than naturalistic forms. Cross stitch is often charted; the embroiderer follows a chart that indicates the correct colors to use for the pattern.

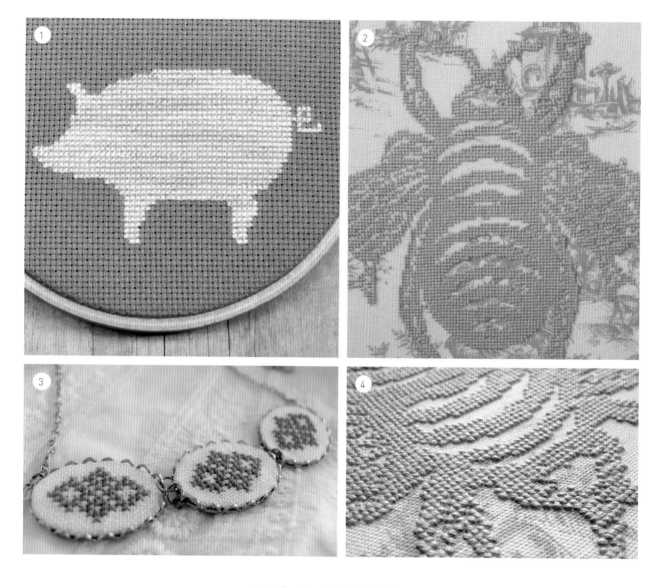

There is no historical or archaeological evidence of the origins of cross-stitch embroidery. It is known that in 6th- and 7th-century eastern Europe, peasants decorated household items with geometric and floral cross-stitch designs. These designs were passed down through the generations from mother to daughter and are still found in pattern books today. One of the earliest surviving pieces of cross stitch is by an English girl called Jane Bastocke. Dated 1598, it is a sampler made up of animal and floral motifs and an alphabet.

Cross stitch came into its own during the 17th century in Europe with the working of samplers. These were small pieces stitched in the form of a prayer or a moral saying. Books with cross-stitch patterns became popular in Europe and America; they were used as educational tools to teach young girls the needlework skills that were essential for making clothing and household linens. The patterns included purses, cushions, fire screens, pin cushions, and footstool tops. During the 18th century pattern books became more complicated, and by the second half of the century, cross-stitched landscapes had become popular.

By the 19th century cross stitching had become a subject that was taught at school in the UK, and practiced by girls and women from all social classes. Interest in samplers dwindled by the end of the century owing to the new craze for Berlin wool work (see page 67).

Cross stitching was rediscovered in the 1960s, when it became a popular technique for embellishing household linens and framed wall decorations. Kits from this period took cross stitch back to its roots by offering the embroiderer copies of traditional samplers that were worked from charts.

Today, cross stitching, with fresh, new designs, has become popular with the younger generation. The current trend is for "subversive cross stitch," involving risqué designs. These often use the traditional sampler style of work but with retro images and sayings intended to shock the viewer.

1. Cross stitch worked in stranded cottons on evenweave fabric *by Tina Fitzpatrick.*
2 and 4. Cross stitch worked in stranded cottons on linen toile de jouy *by Sophie Simpson.*
3. Cross stitch necklace worked in stranded cottons on linen *by Natalka Pavlysh.*
5. Cross stitch worked in stranded cottons on Aida *by Kimberly Scola.*

CROSS-STITCH PRIMER

PLANNING

Cross stitch is a counted-thread technique; it involves working a series of crosses in a range of colors to create a picture. The crosses are typically worked at right angles to each other.

Usually, you follow a chart to create a detailed shaded image. If you are not using a chart, plan a design before you start, working out colors and shades; this will make the stitching easier and more enjoyable.

THREADS

For cross stitch, you generally use stranded cottons, which come in a range of colors and shades and are therefore suitable for creating detailed and realistic pictures.

Stranded cottons have six strands in each length. You can stitch with all six or separate them to work with fewer strands. The number of strands you use in the needle is up to you and the design. If you want to create fine lines or delicate pieces of cross stitch, use just one or two strands in the needle. The more threads used in the needle, the darker and denser the design will be. For stronger lines, try using more threads in the needle.

However many strands you use, make sure that you strand them first—pull out each separate strand and then put them back together; this ensures they stay flat.

STITCHES

If following a chart, you will need to refer to the key to see which colors can be used where and when. A cross stitch consists of two stitches worked at right angles, one of which sits on top of the other. All of the stitches are the same size when working on an evenweave fabric.

There are also partwork cross stitches, which are useful for achieving shapes where a whole cross is not required, and for outlining stitches. These are:

- half cross stitch
- three-quarter cross stitch
- backstitch

Half cross stitch allows you to make shapes that are smoother than with regular cross stitches, so they are useful for creating curves.

Three-quarter cross stitch can be used when a strong design line is in the middle of a cross. You can work three-quarters of the cross in one color and the other quarter in another color.

Backstitch is used to outline cross-stitch designs. It creates crisp lines that are not possible with crosses. Work the backstitch outline once the cross-stitch design is finished.

Holbein stitch is used to outline motifs and areas of a design.

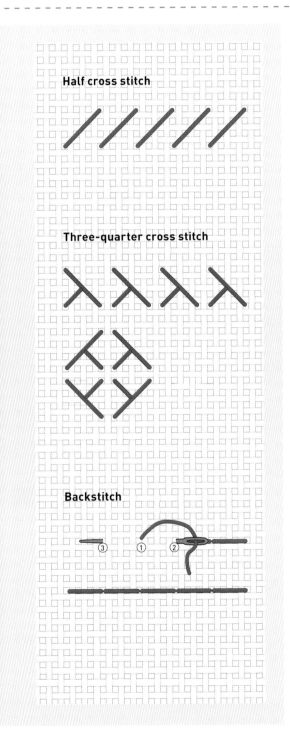

Half cross stitch

Three-quarter cross stitch

Backstitch

③   ①   ②

1

1. Cross-stitch designs worked in stranded cottons on linen *by Sophie Simpson.*

Counted Surface Embroidery

CROSS STITCH
— TUTORIAL —

Cross stitch is a basic stitch by which a design is worked in a series of even-sized crosses. Details are achieved by working the crosses in a range of colors.

Materials
- Evenweave or Aida fabric
- Stranded cottons
- Tapestry needle
- Cross-stitch chart
- Embroidery scissors

Step 1

Bring the needle up at 1 and work a diagonal stitch over the fabric. Then bring the needle up at 2 and work a stitch in the opposite direction. This will create a cross. You can work the crosses over two, three, or four threads, depending on the design.

Step 2

Work a second cross next to the first one; the second stitch shares the holes with the first cross stitch. Work the crosses in a consistent way. It does not matter whether the top thread comes from the bottom right or left, as long as you pick one direction and stick to it.

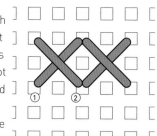

Step 3

Following your chart, work each cross and row in the same way, making sure that all of the top stitches are worked in the same direction.

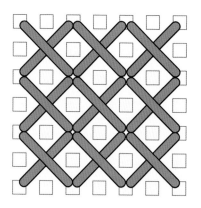

TIP

Work a complete cross before moving on to the next one. This is easier than working half crosses and going back to complete them. Complete crosses are also easier to unpick if you make a mistake.

ASSISI STITCH
— TUTORIAL —

Assisi is an alternative to cross stitch (see facing page). Space is left for a motif and the background filled with cross stitches. The motif is outlined with a Holbein stitch, which is normally worked in a dark color to add definition to the design.

Materials
- Evenweave fabric
- Tapestry needle
- Threads
- Embroidery scissors

Step 1

Work Holbein stitch around the motif. To do this, work a running stitch, counting the holes of the fabric to keep the length of the stitches and the spaces between them consistent. When you have completed this, work back along the row, filling in the spaces with a second group of running stitches.

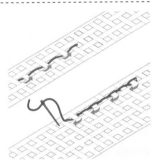

Step 2

You can work any detail inside the motif using surface-embroidery stitches. Then work the background in cross stitch, half cross stitch, or three-quarter cross stitch, depending on the design (see page 106).

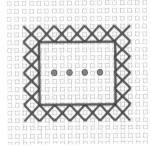

Step 3

Outline the whole shape in Holbein stitch to finish off the piece; this acts as a border to encase the piece of embroidery.

HEATHER GRAY

PROFILE

Heather is inspired by her grandmother, now in her nineties, who has been creating beautiful sewing and embroidery all her life. She has never used a pattern or, if she did, it was a pattern she had designed; she was an artist long before what she was doing was considered art.

Heather also finds inspiration from her grandmother's linen closet, vintage books, and nature. Some days her mind is racing with ideas. She finds it helpful to keep a sketchbook and notepad with her so she can quickly put her ideas on paper as they pop up. Later, she refines them and starts the process of creating a rough pattern. She prides herself on taking a fresh approach to needlepoint, which has always been perceived as a very traditional, even "stuffy," craft.

"I try to keep things fun, never too serious."

"Color changes everything. For example, it can make a traditional pattern feel more modern and vice versa."

When developing her designs, Heather often begins with sketches and then moves to the computer to refine the design. After generating a rough draft of the pattern, she stitches each design. While stitching, she often tweaks the design. The completed piece is used as the template for the patterns, canvases, and kits.

Heather usually finds selecting the colors for a design the most challenging step. How a design is colored can totally change the look of a piece—it can make it or break it. Some designs need high contrast while others require subtle contrast. For example, it can make a traditional pattern feel more modern and vice versa. Finding the perfect balance is not always an easy task.

①

②

③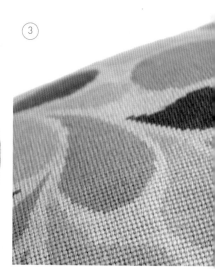

1. Butterfly cushion worked in tent stitch on canvas.
2. Owl worked in tent stitch on specially made wooden disk.
3. Close-up of retro paisley kit, worked on canvas.
4. Union Jack flag worked in tent stitch on specially made wooden disk.
5. Las Vegas cushion worked on canvas, stitched in Silk & Ivory threads.

She likes to experiment on alternative materials—for example, she has developed a line of wooden laser-cut blanks designed especially for needlepoint. These fun little projects can be made into jewelry, key chains, Christmas ornaments, and all kinds of other things.

For technique, Heather uses tent stitch on all of her pieces. She finds it gives her the best coverage and most consistent slant on her stitching. Heather works on Zweigart Mono Deluxe Canvas and Silk & Ivory yarn. She tries to stitch for several hours every day—she loves needlepoint and finds it to be very relaxing. Heather completes most of her designs in one to three months.

Specialty
Needlepoint with a modern twist

Inspired by
Her grandmother's sewing, embroidery, quilting, and crochet projects

Experiments with
Different media, such as laser-cut wood and acrylic

Most challenging project
For every project, choosing the right colors

Top tip
Don't skimp when you are buying needlepoint supplies.

Shop
www.modernneedleworks.etsy.com

Counted Surface Embroidery

CHAPTER 3
EMBELLISHMENT

Embellishments, such as beads and ribbons, are often added to embroideries or textiles to add interest. A number of techniques can be used to add delicate highlights and focal points. Ribbon work and beadwork can also be used on their own to create beautiful, textured pieces of art. The silk ribbons used to create ribbon embroidery and the beads in beadwork are often admired for their stunning colors and textures.

1. A combination of reverse appliqué, surface stitching, and beadwork, worked on a printed cotton, embroidered with stranded cottons *by Zinaida Kazban*.

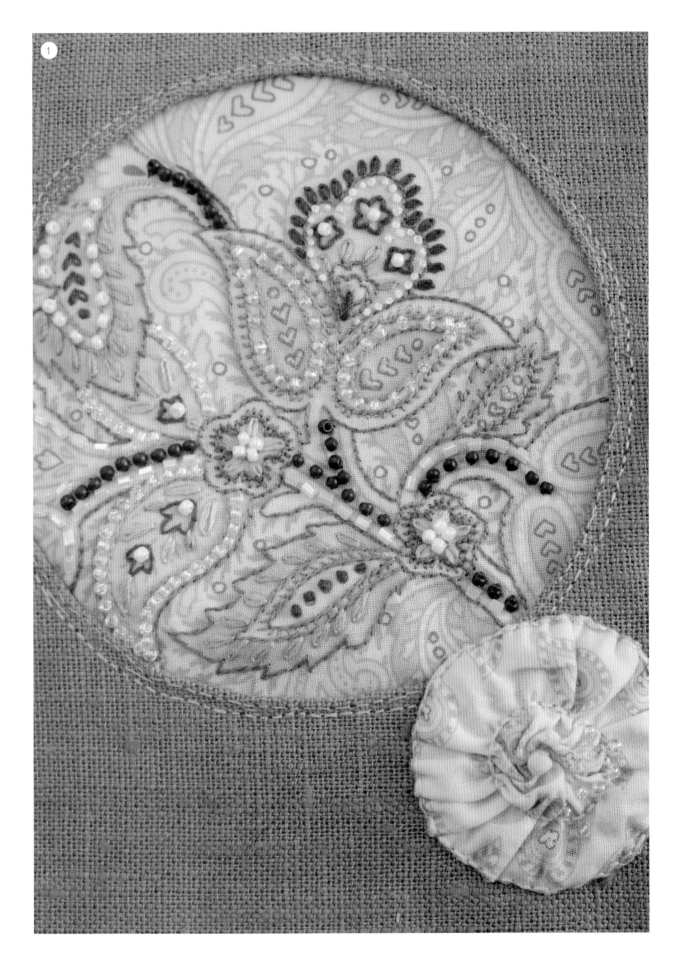

1. Buttons embroidered with threads and beads *by Cécile Franconie.*
2. Ribbon embroidery worked on linen *by Lana Rabinovich.*
3. Monogram worked in a range of beads, with ribbon work and metal thread flowers, on a linen background *by Sophie Long.*

4. Beads, sequins, and jewels hand embroidered on a printed cotton background *by Sophie Long*.
5. Beaded brooch worked on a felt grounded with Nymo thread *by Diana L. Grygo*.

1. Bead embroidery using silamide *by Andrea Adams*.
2. Assorted embellishments hand embroidered on a canvas *by Lisa Giorgi*.
3. Hand-beaded lace appliqué *by Angela Souza*.

3

BEADWORK

Beading is a popular embellishment on clothing, household items, shoes, and bags. Modern beads and gemstones are available in a wide array of shapes, sizes, colors, and materials, encouraging creativity in jewelry making and the customization of clothing. Most embroiderers have a stash of embellishments that can be utilized in their projects.

Beaded embroidery has been used in most cultures for personal adornment for thousands of years. Beads fashioned from seashells, seeds, bones, and other natural objects were used to embellish clothing as long ago as 3,000 B.C.

Some of the first-known examples of beaded embroidery were produced in medieval times (5th to 15th centuries); they were used for German church vestments. Because most of the beadwork at that time was created using costly precious gemstones, its use was limited to ecclesiastical purposes.

In the 14th century, the glass houses of Murano in Italy started to produce beads made of glass, and beaded embroideries became more common. By the 16th century, embroidery had become more extravagant and dressmakers embroidered clothing so densely and elaborately with beads that they began to resemble mosaics. A variety of items, including purses, tiny boxes, and small pictures, were also embellished with beading.

During the Elizabethan period (1558–1603), embroidery was renowned for its ornate embellishments using gold and silver threads, and also beads. As well as being used on clothing, beading was found on a variety of household items from baskets to home furnishings.

With the development of technology and industry in the 19th century, a greater range of beads became available. It is still possible to get semi-precious stone beads and crystals, which are often used on haute-couture clothing but a wide range of economical beads can also be found. Some shops specialize in selling beads made from a range of materials, including glass, plastic, and metal, making beadwork affordable for every embroiderer.

②

③

TIP
Ensure that you get the correct size of needle to pass through your beads to avoid damaging them.

Embellishment

BEADWORK PRIMER

TOOLS

There is a huge selection of beads available. Pick beads that suit your design and the purpose of your bead embroidery. Beads and other tools you will need include:

Needles Select the size according to the beads you will be using.

Thread This needs to be strong and of a color that will blend in with the beads. Nymo thread is ideal.

Beeswax Always run your thread through beeswax to strengthen it.

Beading mat or velvet board A mat or board will help keep your beads in one place before you sew them down; the surface pile should stop the beads from rolling around.

Glass beads Use small round beads, often called seed beads. These come in a range of sizes from 5/0 to 24/0; the bigger the number, the smaller the bead. Glass beads can be opaque, metallic, transparent, iridescent, or silver-lined.

Bugle beads These tube-shaped glass beads are longer than seed beads. Bugle beads range in size from approximately 1/16 to 1½ in/1 to 35 mm.

Sequins These are disk-shaped and come in a range of sizes.

Backing When working bead embroidery it is best to back the fabric to support the weight of a large amount of beads. Synthetic fabrics such as imitation suedes are a good choice.

STITCHES

Many stitches can be used to secure beads. When deciding which stitches to work, consider how the piece will be used. If you are applying beads to clothing or another item that is going to be used a lot, you will need to work sufficient stitches to hold the beads securely and prevent them from catching on other objects.

If you are applying beads to a piece of embroidery that will be framed, you can get away with fewer securing stitches. The stitches most often used for securing beads are:

- running stitch
- backstitch
- satin stitch
- couching

The technique you use will depend upon the type of bead, and how many beads you are attaching.

Running stitch with single bead Bring the needle up and thread on the bead, then take the needle down on the other side of the bead, so that the bead is sitting on the fabric.

Running stitch with bead groups The same method can be used for two or more beads. When you bring the needle up, thread on the number of beads you require, then take the needle down where the length of beads ends.

Running stitch with sequins Sequins can also be applied individually or in groups, and can be combined with beads. Bring the needle up at the edge of a sequin and take the needle down into the hole. The number of stitches you work around the sequin is optional. Coming up on the outside of the sequin and then going down into the hole gives a neater finish.

1. Beadwork using KO thread on Stitch N Shape *by Amy Wallace.*
2. Beading, free-motion machine embroidery, and hand embroidery using cotton floss and sewing thread on batting, cotton, and reclaimed fabric *by Monika Kinner-Whalen.*
3. Beadwork using KO thread on Stitch N Shape *by Amy Wallace.*

Running stitch with beads and sequins Place the sequin onto the needle before threading on the bead, slide these down onto the fabric, then take the needle back down into the sequin. The bead anchors the sequin and covers the stitches. Use a bead that is slightly larger than the hole of the sequin; if it isn't, the sequin will come off.

Backstitch with sequins Sequins can also be sewn down using a backstitch. Follow the same method as for backstitch with beads and sequins, below. You can set your sequins side by side or overlapping.

Backstitch with beads and sequins Bring the needle up and thread on the first bead, then take the needle down to the design line in the opposite direction. Come up again one bead's length away from the previous bead and thread on the next bead.

Satin stitch with bead groups Blocks of beads can be worked using running stitch to create a satin-stitch cluster (see page 184). Start in the middle of the shape to set the angle, then work outward to complete the shape.

Couching To couch beads (see pages 37 and 50) you first need to thread up your desired bead combination. Plan your pattern and color combinations, thread them all up, and use a different thread to work a stitch between each bead as a securing stitch. The beads can be couched individually or in groups.

BEADWORK ON CANVAS
— TUTORIAL —

You can do beadwork on canvas, which is a strong openweave mesh. Each bead takes the place of a tent stitch (see page 78). Use beads to completely cover the surface of the canvas or combine them with background stitches worked in tent stitch. To design your own piece, use graph paper to produce a shape or repeat pattern. Use the squares of the graph paper to represent the seed beads. Colored pencils are a quick way of creating a pattern.

Materials
- Strong thread that blends with the color of the beads
- Beeswax
- Double canvas
- Beading needle
- Seed beads
- Beading mat

Step 1

Wax the thread to strengthen and smooth it. Fasten the thread by working two small stitches, or tying a knot, and bringing the needle up through a hole in the canvas.

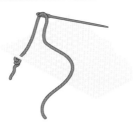

Step 2

Thread the needle through a bead and push the bead down to lie on the canvas. Take the needle down into the hole next to your bead, in line with your first stitch. Add another bead in the same way.

Step 3

Continue to work this stitch, each time threading on a new bead or beads. Follow a chart if you are recreating a pattern or picture.

Step 4

Once you have applied a row of beads, slide the needle back through the beads to secure them. Continue with your next row.

1 and 2. Beadwork, stumpwork, and appliqué using beads and stranded cottons on muslin *by Zinaida Kazban*.

BEADING ON A LOOM

— TUTORIAL —

For this beadwork you need a loom. The loom holds the warp threads across it. These threads are parallel and under tension so that strips of beads can be woven across them with the weft thread. Beading on a loom creates pieces of beading that are not attached to fabric; the threads hold all the beads together. Before you start, plan your design on graph paper.

Materials
- Loom
- Warp and weft thread: strong but fine enough to fit through the beads you are using at least four times
- Beading needle
- Beads of consistent size
- Embroidery scissors

Step 1

To thread up the loom, attach a warp thread to one of the anchoring nails. Bring the thread up and ensure it lies in a slot. Pass it to the other end of the loom and fit it in the corresponding slot. Wrap the thread around the nail, bring it up to the next slot and take the thread back across the loom to its corresponding slot on the other side. Continue to pass warp threads back and forth until you have one more than you need for your design.

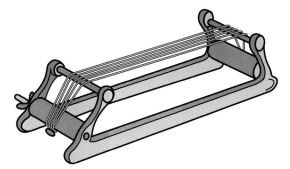

Step 2

Cut about 1 yd/1 m of weft thread and tie it to the outside warp thread, leaving a tail of approximately 6 in/15 cm. (If you are right-handed, tie the knot to the left warp; if you are left-handed, tie it to the right warp.)

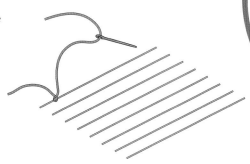

TIP
If you need to change the warp thread, allow for a tail of approximately 6 in/15 cm at the end of the row. You will weave this in when the piece is finished. Tie a new weft thread onto the outside warp thread, again leaving a tail of 6 in/15 cm, and continue.

Step 3

Thread the first row of the design onto your beading needle, sliding the beads down the weft thread to the knot. Bring the weft thread under the warp thread and then push up the beads using your fingers so that you get one bead between every two warp threads. Holding the beads in place, pass the needle back through all of the beads, making sure that the weft thread passes above the warp threads.

Step 4

Continue using the method in step 3 to weave the design. Weave in the tails of the weft threads; if possible, undo the knot that you made at the beginning of the weft thread. Thread this tail into a needle and pass it through a few beads to about the middle of the row. Pass the needle through the remaining beads in that row or move down to the row below and pass the remaining tail through the beads.

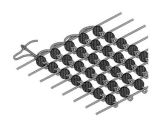

Step 5

To tie off the warp threads, cut the threads close to the nails and remove the work from the loom. Thread each warp thread into a needle and take it back into the piece; make sure you weave it in going around both warp and weft threads to ensure it is secure. Tie a knot around a junction of the warp and weft threads; then continue to pass it under several beads before cutting off the remaining thread.

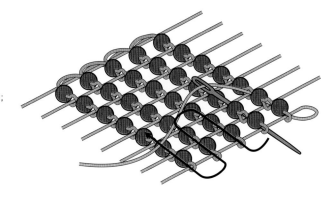

RIBBON WORK

Ribbon work can either be worked on its own
to create stunning textural embroideries or
combined with crewelwork, cross stitch, and canvas
work (needlepoint). Ribbon embroidery is an effective
technique that can be used for embellishing a range
of items, including wall hangings, framed pieces,
clothing, bags, and shoes.

Ribbon work became popular during the French Rococo period (c. 1700–1750). During this time, the dresses of royalty and court ladies were embellished with ribbon-work sprays. This floral embroidery was created by professionals and kept very much within the French royal family. The ladies of the British court soon caught on to this trend and adopted the use of rosettes and ribbon work to embellish their dresses.

During the later part of the 18th and early 19th centuries, ribbon became less common as other forms of embellishment grew in popularity. Ribbon embroidery was revived somewhat with the success of the French couturier Charles Worth (1826–1895), who transformed the fashion industry. In the early 1900s, ribbon work gained favor when it appeared on men's waistcoats, sewing accessories, crazy quilts, purses, clothing, and household objects.

The popularity of ribbon work rose and fell during the 20th century. In the 1990s, there was a great revival of interest when embroiderers in Australia began to reintroduce this delicate technique. Silk ribbon embroidery became fashionable not only on clothes but also on ladies' small handbags, caps, and gloves. It was also used to embellish plain shawls and blankets, as well as other homewares.

Ribbon embroidery remains a popular embroidery technique in a number of countries. The style of ribbon work has not changed that much; the nature of the technique lends itself to pretty floral designs. The ribbons are hand dyed and produced in beautiful tones and shades. However, the number of companies producing silk ribbons is fairly limited, so the ribbons can be quite hard to find and relatively expensive.

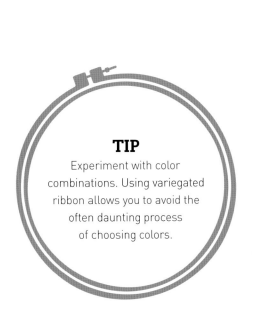

TIP
Experiment with color combinations. Using variegated ribbon allows you to avoid the often daunting process of choosing colors.

2

Embellishment

STARTING A THREAD
— TUTORIAL —

When starting a thread, bear in mind that the ribbon should pass through the eye of the needle easily. The most popular sizes of ribbon are ⅛ in/3 mm, ¼ in/6 mm, and ½ in/13 mm.

Materials
- Silk ribbon
- Chenille needle
- Embroidery scissors

Step 1

Cut a length of ribbon about 12 in/30 cm long. Cut the ribbon diagonally to make it easier to thread. Take the point of the needle through the ribbon about ½ in/13 mm from the end.

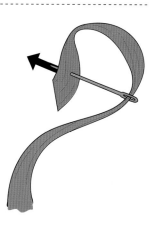

Step 2

Keep hold of the tail with your other hand and push the needle through to create a knot close to the needle.

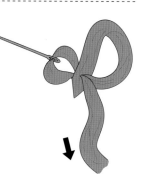

Step 3

Pull the needle with one hand and hold on to the ribbon with the other. This should slide the knot up to the eye of the needle. A small knot can also be created at the other end of the ribbon. Now the ribbon is ready to be worked.

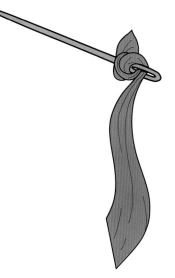

TIP
Use short lengths of ribbon so that you don't pass it through the fabric too often—this can cause fraying. After bringing the needle through the fabric, use a spare needle to stroke the ribbon close to the fabric, to smooth out any damage.

WOVEN WHEEL

— TUTORIAL —

You can create ribbon roses by working a woven wheel using ribbons. If you want a large rose, ensure that you are using ¼ in/6 mm or ½ in/13 mm ribbon. For large roses, you may wish to work seven or nine spokes instead of the five mentioned in Step 1. You can use longer lengths of ribbon because you do not need to enter the fabric often.

Materials
- Fabric (any)
- Embroidery thread that matches the ribbon
- Embroidery needle
- Ribbon
- Chenille needle
- Embroidery scissors

Step 1

Thread the embroidery needle with one strand of embroidery thread matching the ribbon color, and work five evenly spaced spokes in a circle on your fabric. Thread the chenille needle with the ribbon, bring it up close to the center in between two spokes and then take it under the first spoke.

Step 2

Go over the next spoke and under the one after. Continue working around the wheel, under and over the spokes. Keep the tension fairly loose. The ribbon does not pierce the fabric.

Step 3

Once you have completely covered the spokes, take the ribbon down to the back of the fabric.

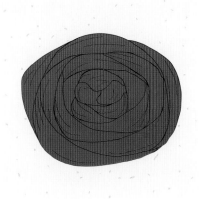

TIP
If you do not have enough ribbon for the whole rose or wish to shade it or change the color, take the needle down and secure the ribbon at the back. Bring up the new ribbon where the last one finished, and continue to weave.

STRAIGHT STITCH

——◦—— TUTORIAL ——◦——

Straight stitch is a very simple stitch. You can work it at a range of lengths, depending on what you wish to create. For example, work longer stitches for leaves than for petals.

Materials
- Fabric (any)
- Ribbon
- Embroidery scissors
- Chenille needle
- Spare needle

Step 1

Bring the chenille needle up with the ribbon attached and take it down at the desired stitch length. Before pulling the ribbon flat on the fabric, place a spare needle in the loop to gently lift the stitch from the fabric and control where it enters the fabric.

Step 2

With the spare needle in place to stop the ribbon from pulling tight and lying next to the fabric, pull the threaded needle so that the ribbon touches the spare needle.

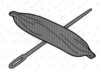

Step 3

Gently remove the spare needle to use it for the next straight stitch.

TIP

Store ribbons on reels to prevent them from creasing before you work with them. If ribbons do crease, you can gently iron them before you start work.

LOOPED STRAIGHT STITCH
——•— TUTORIAL —•——

Looped straight stitch is similar to straight stitch but the stitches are left with excess ribbon on the top of the fabric. This extra ribbon forms a loop that can be left as it is, or you can work a French knot in stranded cotton in the middle to create a flower.

Materials
- Fabric (any)
- Ribbon
- Chenille needle
- Embroidery needle
- Mellor
- Embroidery thread
- Embroidery scissors

Step 1

Thread the chenille needle with the ribbon. Bring it up through the fabric and take it back down, but before pulling the ribbon loop tight, place a mellor through it. This raises the stitch higher from the fabric than the needle used in straight stitch (see opposite). Gently pull the ribbon down.

Step 2

Bring up the needle ready to work the next stitch. You can then slide out the mellor and work the next stitch, with the mellor ready to place for the following stitch.

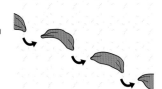

Step 3

Work a French knot (see page 33) in the middle of the stitch using the embroidery needle and embroidery thread.

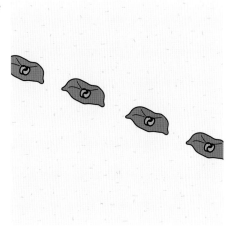

RIBBON STITCH

— TUTORIAL —

Ribbon stitch creates a straight stitch with a curl at the end. There is a lot of flexibility with this stitch; you can work it in any width of ribbon. Take care when working ribbon stitch to ensure that the loop you create is not pulled to the back of the fabric. This can happen if you pull the remaining ribbon when you start the next stitch.

Materials
- Fabric (any)
- Ribbons
- Chenille needle
- Spare needle or mellor
- Embroidery scissors

Step 1

Bring the ribbon threaded–chenille needle up and lay the ribbon flat on the fabric to determine the stitch length. Take the needle down through ribbon and fabric, then place a spare needle or mellor in the loop to gently lift it and create a curl.

Step 2

With the needle or mellor in place to stop the ribbon from pulling tight and lying next to the fabric, bring up the needle ready to work the next stitch. Make sure you work gently.

Step 3

Gently remove the spare needle to use it for the next stitch.

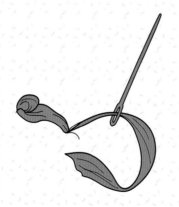

TIP
Ribbon stitch is very effective for creating leaves. Use variegated ribbons to add depth to your piece.

GATHERED RIBBON

— TUTORIAL —

Gathered ribbon is an element that is worked off the fabric and attached once it is gathered. The size of the ribbon will have an effect on the finished piece. It is best to start with ½ in/13 mm ribbons because they are not too fiddly to work with.

Materials
- Ribbon
- Embroidery needle
- Embroidery scissors
- Thread to match ribbon
- Fabric (any)

Step 1

Cut approximately 4 in/10 cm of ribbon. Using a small embroidery needle and matching thread, work a row of tiny running stitches along the ribbon edge. Ensure that the running stitches are close to the edge so you will have as much ribbon as possible visible once it is gathered.

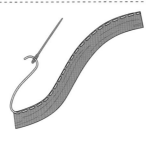

Step 2

Once you have worked the running stitches, pull the thread to gather up the ribbon and form a circle, easing it into shape with your fingers. Where the ends meet, work some oversewing stitches to secure the raw edges.

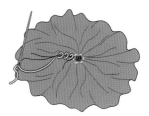

Step 3

Turn the gathering over so that the oversewn raw edges are at the back, and sew the gathered ribbon onto the fabric, using a couple of stab stitches in the middle (see page 36). It should be raised from the fabric.

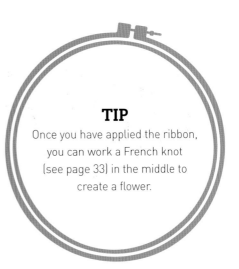

TIP

Once you have applied the ribbon, you can work a French knot (see page 33) in the middle to create a flower.

THE LONE BEADER
(DIANA L. GRYGO)

The Lone Beader makes bead embroidery: the art of stitching tiny glass seed beads to felt, two to three at a time, using a needle and strong nylon thread. She also uses beaded fringe and layered beaded backstitch techniques to create dimension and realism.

Most of the Lone Beader's work has been inspired by classic cars, city scenes, and dogs. She is inspired by vehicles most because they take us to new places, but dogs keep us company when we arrive!

> "I am attracted to all things vintage with modern design elements and I am constantly thinking of ways to incorporate these ideas into my beadwork."

The Lone Beader usually starts out with a series of sketches that she modifies and resizes using Photoshop. She prints out her finished sketch and creates a template, which she uses to cut out a number of felt layers, which she stitches together.

Afterward, she simply stitches beads to the felt, adding beaded fringe or other textural elements as needed. She stitches beads to felt, Ultrasuede, vinyl, or canvas using 3 in/8 cm beading needles and Nymo thread. She uses Japanese size 15 seed beads for the dog pins and larger sizes for the beaded paintings.

Beaded dog pins and pendants take the Lone Beader approximately six to ten hours to create, depending on the breed. Larger beaded paintings can take from two to ten months to complete, depending on the size and complexity of the piece. The most challenging process for every piece is creating the felt foundation. She typically cuts out between

① ②

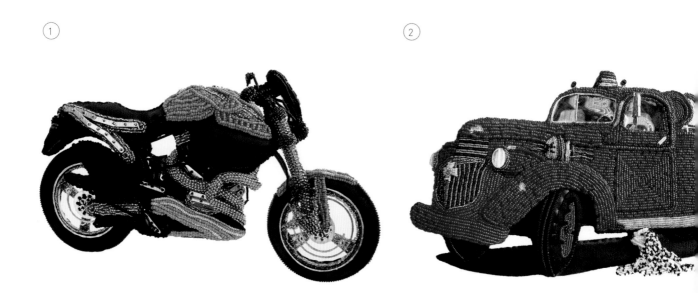

"Discover and perfect the techniques that work best for you, then innovate, create, inspire."

five and twelve layers of felt for each subject in a manner that will add substantial relief to the finished piece. The larger the piece, the more involved this process is, and the longer it takes.

The Lone Beader exhibits at the Cambridge Art Association in Cambridge, MA, USA. She also enters national juried shows.

Specialty
Beadwork on raised pieces of felt

Inspired by
Dogs and classic cars

Experiments with
3D objects

Most challenging aspect
Preparing the felt before beads can be applied

Top tip
Use short lengths of thread and work in small sections; if you make a mistake, you can undo the small section not the whole piece.

Shop
www.etsy.com/shop/thelonebeader
www.zazzle.com/thelonebeader

CHAPTER 4

STUMPWORK

Stumpwork is a broad category of embroidery that encompasses all techniques that are raised from the fabric. Traditional stumpwork pieces often include figures, animals, and floral elements. Embroiderers use padding and wire to create elements that are separate from the fabric, adding a three-dimensional aspect to the piece. Needlelace is one of the main stitches used in stumpwork (see pages 158–65); it can be worked in a variety of stitches to create a pattern that resembles crochet or knitting.

1. Stumpwork frog worked on a linen background *by Sophie Long*.
2. Stumpwork critters worked on a painted and partly stitched canvas *by Sarah Homfray*.
3. Stumpwork figure worked on a painted and surface-embroidered background *by Sophie Long*.

Stumpwork

137

1. Stumpwork figure worked using a range of fabrics and techniques, including needlelace on the dress *by Mimi Chan*.
2. Stumpwork and machine embroidery using rayon threads on wool *by Lana Rabinovich*.
3. Stumpwork and appliqué using cotton and wool on linen *by Kei Shinano*.
4. Stumpwork using cotton and metallic threads on linen, cotton, silk dupion, and Tana Lawn *by Laura Mason*.

RAISED AND DETACHED ELEMENTS

Stumpwork is a type of three-dimensional or raised embroidery that is currently enjoying a revival. Some people still work it in its original historical themes but it can also be worked in more contemporary designs. The elements are often worked separately and are wired to stand away from the fabric. Once worked, they are applied to the main fabric.

Stumpwork dates back to the 15th century when it was used for ecclesiastical embellishments: embroiderers used it for padding small areas of crewelwork (see pages 24–33). In Britain in the mid-17th century, the technique became popular in its own right for domestic purposes. It was during this period that some of the most spectacular examples of stumpwork were produced. Many of these pieces were pictorial and depicted pastoral and historical scenes, often with beautifully dressed kings and queens as the central figures.

Many of the later designs included elements that were raised from the surface; these were either worked completely detached from the embroidery and applied later, or they could be worked on the fabric—but not all of the elements were stitched down. It is the contrast between these raised elements and flat surface stitches that gives stumpwork its playful feel.

The popularity of stumpwork dwindled by the end of the 17th century but it underwent a revival in the late 20th century. This was largely thanks to the efforts of Barbara Hirst from England; in the 1980s she rediscovered this form of embroidery and started to demonstrate and teach it around the world. A typical modern example of stumpwork contains freestanding padded pieces of embroidery lifted off the fabric with the use of florists' wire.

The detached and raised stitches in stumpwork can also be worked with other surface stitches to give a slightly different feel. Stumpwork is often very effective when worked alongside appliqué—after applying base fabrics, the raised elements are worked over the top.

Stumpwork raised and detached elements can be worked on framed pieces of embroidery and used to create raised elements on items such as brooches and jewelry. Working with jewelry requires great care because often the wire is quite fine and therefore delicate, but the results can be extremely attractive.

TIP
As elements are detached from the fabric, make sure you keep them safe until they are ready to be applied.

3

WIRED EDGE

— TUTORIAL —

To create raised parts of a stumpwork design, you can work a wired edge around a shape, which allows the shape to bend. With a wired edge, you can use a decorative fabric, for example, printed cotton or fine organza, or you can fill the wired shape with stitching—typically long and short stitch (see page 30).

Materials
- Pencil
- Fabric (any)
- Embroidery scissors
- Ring frame
- Paper-covered wire
- Stranded cotton
- Embroidery needle
- Stiletto
- Fabric scissors
- Wire cutters

Step 1

Draw your shape on the fabric and secure it in a ring frame. Leaving a tail of wire of at least 2 in/5 cm, place the wire onto the design and work an overcast stitch around the edge. Make sure that there are no gaps where the wire is visible. This overcasting is called trailing.

Step 2

Finish off the thread at the base where the two wires meet. With a new thread, work buttonhole stitch over the top of the trailing: take the needle down outside the shape, bring it up inside, then through the loop outside.

Step 3

Cast off the thread. Work decorative stitches inside the shape, if required. Remove the fabric from the frame and carefully cut out the shape, trimming off a few millimeters at a time so as to avoid cutting any of the stitches.

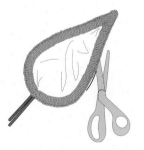

Step 4

With a stiletto, make a small hole in the embroidery where you wish the wired shape to go, and push the wires through the fabric. Bend the wires back onto the fabric and work some securing stitches to hold it in place. Make sure that the stitches are small so they do not show too much. Trim off the excess wires.

STITCHED WIRED EDGE
━━ TUTORIAL ━━

Creating a stitched wire edge is similar to making a wired edge (see facing page), but is slightly more time consuming because you also embroider the shape. Long and short stitch (see page 30) is the most common stitch to use because you can shade the design; this is very effective for petals and leaves.

Materials
- Pencil
- Fabric (any)
- Ring frame
- Paper-covered wire
- Stranded cottons in a range of shades
- Embroidery scissors
- Embroidery needle
- Stiletto
- Fabric scissors
- Wire cutters

Step 1

Draw your shape onto the fabric and secure it in a ring frame. Leaving a tail of wire of at least 2 in/5 cm, place the wire onto the design and work an overcast stitch around the edge. Make sure that there are no gaps where the wire is visible. This overcasting is called trailing.

Step 2

Finish off the thread at the base. Embroider inside the shape with long and short stitch. Tuck up the first row into the trailing so there is no gap where the stitching meets the wire. With a new thread, work buttonhole stitch over the top of the trailing: take the needle down outside the shape, bring it up inside, then through the loop outside.

Step 3

Cast off the thread. Remove the fabric from the frame and carefully cut out the shape, trimming off a few millimeters at a time so as to avoid cutting any of the stitches.

Step 4

With a stiletto, make a small hole in the embroidery where you wish the wired shape to go, and push the wires through the fabric. Bend the wires back onto the fabric and work some securing stitches to hold it in place. Make sure that the stitches are small so they do not show too much. Trim off the excess wires.

SLIPS

— TUTORIAL —

Slips are detached shapes that are applied to a piece of embroidery. They can be plain fabric, canvas worked, or embroidered; the size will vary depending on your design.

Materials
- Fabric (any) or canvas
- Embroidery needle
- Sewing thread
- Embroidery scissors
- Padding
- Fabric scissors

Step 1

Work on the design drawn onto the fabric. Use a stitch to suit the design, such as French knots (see page 33) long and short stitch (page 30), or tent stitch (page 78). Use sewing thread to stitch around the shape ⅛ in/3 mm away from the design to form a gathering thread.

Step 2

Cut out the slip, leaving approximately ¼ in/6 mm around the stitches.

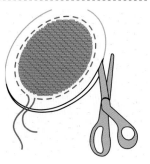

Step 3

Pull up the gathering thread so that all of the loose and fraying edges are pulled to the back and secured by finishing off the thread. Depending on the size of the design, you may wish to add some padding at this stage.

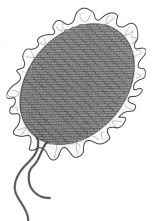

Step 4

Oversew the back of the slip to remove any loose threads and keep the slip tight. Stab-stitch the slip to the embroidery (see page 36) so that the raw edges are on the back.

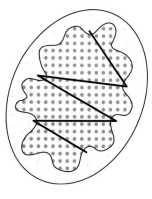

RIBBON-WRAPPED BEAD

⚬— TUTORIAL —⚬

It was very common in 17th-century stumpwork to wrap found objects to create raised elements. Wooden beads make a smooth surface to wrap, ideal for creating a range of fruits. Silk ribbons allow you to be creative with color; look out for variegated ribbons, which can really add depth to your embroidery.

Materials

- Wooden bead with large hole
- Silk ribbon ⅛–¼ in/3–6 mm
- Chenille needle
- Embroidery scissors

Step 1

Thread the ribbon through the eye of the needle. While holding the tail end of the ribbon in one hand, take the needle through the hole of the bead.

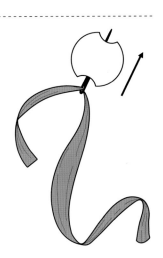

Step 2

Start wrapping the ribbon around the bead, taking the needle through the hole with each wrap. No part of the bead should be visible, so ensure that each wrap of ribbon slightly overlaps the last and is lying smoothly.

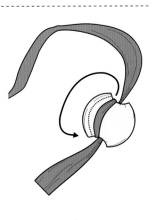

Step 3

Continue until the bead is completely wrapped. The ribbon should be touching where the first and last wrap meet, and all of the bead should be covered.

TIP
White ribbon can be painted using silk paints to achieve the correct color for your design.

Step 4

Take the tail with the needle still attached back through the hole, catching in some of the ribbons inside of the bead to finish it off. These two tails can then be placed back into your needle and be used to secure the wrapped bead onto the embroidery.

DETACHED WOVEN PICOTS

— TUTORIAL —

Detached woven picots are small leaf shapes, attached to the fabric at the base. The tip of the leaf is not attached. You can work detached woven picots in stranded cottons or wools, depending on how delicate you would like them. The maximum length that you can work detached woven picots is ½ in/13 mm. They are attached by only three threads and can become unstable if worked larger.

Materials
- Fabric (any)
- Stranded cotton or wool
- Glass-headed pin
- Embroidery needle
- Embroidery scissors

Step 1

Insert a pin to mark the tip of your leaf and bring it up where you want its base. Bring your threaded needle up to one side of the base, at 1, then take it around the head of the pin at 2, and back down at 3.

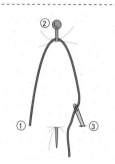

Step 2

Bring the needle back up between 1 and 3, at 4, and take the needle up and around the pin head again. This is your "leaf frame."

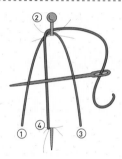

Step 3

Weave the thread backward and forward across the shape, going alternately over and under the threads of your "leaf frame." Push the wraps up to ensure that there are no gaps in between the weaves.

Step 4

When you can no longer fit in any more weaves, take the thread through to the back. Remove the pin from the fabric. The picot will now stand away from the fabric.

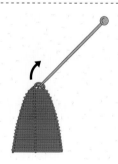

TIP

You can also work picots flat on the fabric. Work the initial three stitches that form the framework for weaving straight into the fabric without a pin. You can also create finer picots by working only two prongs.

RAISED LEAF STITCH
— TUTORIAL —

Raised leaf stitch is a delicate raised surface stitch that lends itself to leaves due to its shape; you can also work five stitches around a circle to create a flower. Raised leaf stitch is worked straight onto background fabric.

Materials
- Scissors
- Card
- Fabric (any)
- Embroidery needle
- Embroidery thread

Step 1

Cut a piece of card ⅛ x 2 in/ 3 x 50 mm. Bring the needle up a third of the way along the card and back down the same hole. Before pulling the thread, place the card in between the loop, ensuring that it remains upright.

Step 2

Work five to eight stitches—the longer the leaf, the more stitches needed. Bring the needle through the fabric up one side of the card, down the other and through the fabric. The stitches should hug the card but not damage it.

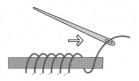

Step 3

Once you have the stitches worked, bring the needle up as if to work the next stitch but slide the needle under the stitches and along the card to the start of the stitches.

Step 4

Gently pull out the card and the stitches will then fall on to the fabric with the needle inside of the loops.

Step 5

Work a stitch around the loops to secure them.

TIP

The final stitch can be worked in a complementary color to create a vein within the leaf pattern.

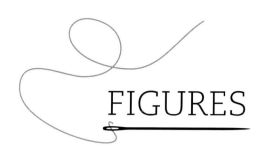

FIGURES

Stumpwork figures are usually worked on an
embroidered background. The body is padded and
dressed in either applied fabric or needlelace clothing.
The face is often the hardest part to get right
since the small size makes it fiddly.

During the 17th century, stumpwork became increasingly elaborate and eventually the human figures began to resemble small dolls. These were dressed in intricate clothing, and the embroiderers often used human and animal hair for beards and hairstyles. The figures were often stitched over a wire frame and then attached to the fabric; this is called a slip. This allowed the creator to make the figures realistic, because items of clothing were worked separately and then applied. The items of clothing were built up from the underwear to outerwear, similar to when dressing a doll. The wire made it possible to lift up the outer clothes to see the undergarments. Most of the clothing on the figures was worked in needlelace, a variation of buttonhole stitch (see pages 158–65). The needlelace was extremely fine and therefore difficult to create.

FIGURES PRIMER

PLANNING

Before you pick up a needle, find an image of the figure you wish to create. Working from a photograph is a good idea because it helps you to achieve the correct proportions.

BACKGROUND

Stumpwork figures are generally placed in the foreground of a design, so it is important to work all of the background first. Some of the elements of a figure are worked separately, so these could be started alongside the background.

BODY

Transfer your design on to the fabric. Take care to apply only the lines that are essential and are not raised from the fabric. For example, do not put the hands on to the fabric because they would be raised from the piece, and then the lines would be visible.

The body is padded with felt first. Make sure that you cut the felt padding to the shape of the body and not to the clothes the figure will wear. The face and neck are usually a cotton lawn, painted if necessary to achieve the correct skin tone. Since the hands are made using stranded cotton, it is a good idea to match the skin to the stranded cotton color, rather than the other way round.

Apply the neck and hands before you dress your figure because these sit underneath the clothing. The face and hair are the last to be applied since these will sit on top of the neck.

CLOTHING

Fabrics are applied to the body to create clothing, and you can also work needlelace items (see pages 158–65). Small pieces of leather work well for shoes (see page 53).

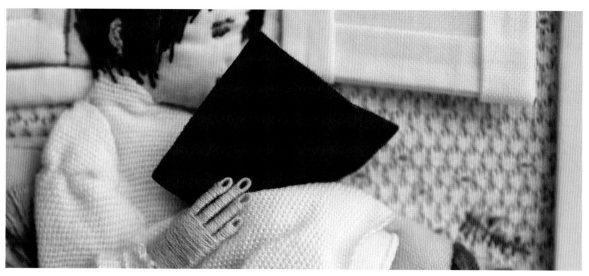

Detail of stumpwork shown on page 138.

BODY

— TUTORIAL —

You need to create a body for your figure before any clothes are applied. The aim is to create realistic forms so that the clothes fit properly. Once the body is padded, you will work the clothes separately and apply them to the figure.

Materials
- Fabric (any)
- Felt—a color that will not show through the clothing fabric/embroideries
- Embroidery needle
- Embroidery scissors
- Wadding or fleece

Step 1

Once you have transferred the design of the figure to the fabric and cut out the felt, start to apply it to the fabric using a stab stitch (see page 36). The needle always comes up in the background fabric and down into the felt.

Step 2

Apply the felt from the neck downward. Start to stuff it using a wadding or fleece material. Take care not to over-pad it. Where you need to add definition, such as the chest or waist, work a backstitch (see page 106).

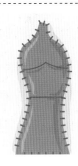

Step 3

Continue stab stitching and stuffing the shape until you have completed the main torso. Work the arms and legs in the same way, again taking care not to over-pad them.

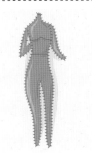

Step 4

You can then apply the fabric for the neck and legs, which should be either clothing or skin-colored fabric. You now have the basic body to which you will add hands and feet before applying the clothes.

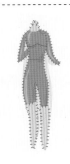

TIP
You can use a mellor to gently push the padding into the shapes and ensure it is smooth and well shaped.

FACE

TUTORIAL

The face is the hardest part of stumpwork. First, paint a fine lawn fabric with watercolors to create the same color as the threads used for the hands, then start to work the face. You can add more paint afterward to add shadows or contours if required.

Materials
- Lawn fabric
- Fabric (any)
- Ring frame
- Embroidery needle
- Embroidery scissors
- Sewing thread
- Wadding or cotton wool
- Mellor or tweezers
- Pencil
- Tracing paper
- Softwood and craft knife
- Water-based glue
- Paintbrush
- Watercolors
- Fabric scissors

Step 1

Transfer the shape of the face on to the first piece of fabric, which is placed in a ring frame. Do this by tracing the shape from the final design. You will stitch the face onto this shape.

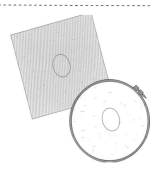

Step 2

Make a slip for the face. Transfer the face outline onto another piece of lawn. Work small running stitches around it, starting at the top of the face. Do not cut off the thread. Cut out the slip, about ¼ in/6 mm outside the stitches and pull the threads gently to gather up the face.

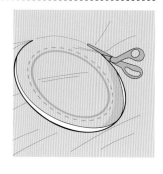

Step 3

Place the slip face down on the fabric and secure it with the thread used to gather the face. Bring the needle up through the fabric on the design line, catch into the slip, and take the needle back down. Start at the top of the head and work downward to the ears, using small stitches.

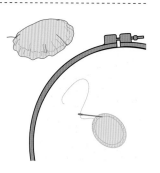

Step 4

Stuff the top of the head with pieces of wadding or cotton wool, using a mellor or tweezers to insert the padding.

Step 5

Draw the facial features on tracing paper and place this over the face as a guide. Work three small stab stitches (see page 36) where the eyes will be: one in the middle and two at the eye sockets.

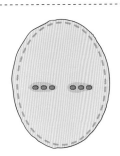

Step 6

Stab stitch around the rest of the face, padding as you go. Pad the cheeks and chin well. Work the final stitches around the face, working an additional stitch for the mouth.

Step 7

Cut a small piece of softwood for the nose. Place the nose on the face and work a couple of stitches across it to keep it in place. With diluted water-based glue and a paintbrush, brush over the stitched outline. Leave it to dry before continuing.

TIP

Drawing the face on tracing paper first helps with placement. Remove the tracing paper before you start stitching.

continued over page

Step 8

Cut out the slip close to the stitches (see Tip), and place it on another piece of lawn (painted if necessary). Draw around the face, leaving a ¼-in/6-mm border. Work small running stitches around the pencil lines and cut out the shape ¼ in/6 mm away from the stitched line. Place this over the face and gather up the stitches by pulling the remaining thread.

Step 9

Lace the back of the face using the remaining thread. Ensure that the face is smooth with no excess fabric. Attach the face to the embroidery with small stab stitches. Start by working a couple of stitches all the way around the face to hold it in place, then go back, working in between those stitches.

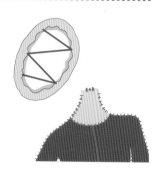

TIP

The first face worked is used as the padding and template for the second piece of fabric (step 8). The stitches up to step 8 are a guide for the facial features in step 10.

Step 10

Work the features on to the face. Use small stab stitches for the eyes and work straight stitches (see page 130) or stem stitches (see page 29) for the mouth and eyebrows. Use watercolor paint to add shadows around the hairline, and make the cheeks rosy.

HAIR
━●━ TUTORIAL ━●━

Once you have worked the face, you can create the hair; the technique will depend on the design of your figure. Is the hair long or short? Straight or curly? Blonde or brown? Use the appropriate thread color and stitch to create the desired effect. If you pad the hair, use a felt that matches the hair color.

Materials
- Fabric (any)
- Threads in appropriate colors—use more than one shade to achieve a natural effect
- Embroidery needle
- Embroidery scissors
- Crochet hook or large needle
- Water-based glue
- Felt padding if needed

Step 1

You can work surface stitches for hair. The stitch you use will depend on the hair type you are trying to create. Use long and short stitch (see page 30) for mid-length to long straight hair. For short, textured hair, work French knots (see page 33) to create texture.

Step 2

To create ringlets, use a large needle or crochet hook and diluted water-based glue. Wrap the thread around the needle and paint a small amount of glue around it.

Step 3

Leave the ringlet to dry, then take it off the needle and sew it on to the embroidery. You can experiment with the number of stitches or try using a combination of stitches to create hair that looks like your design. If you wish to pad the hair, apply a layer of felt in an appropriate color. Work small stab stitches around the felt, then embroidery stitches on top.

HANDS

— TUTORIAL —

Stumpwork hands are made by wrapping paper-covered wire. Owing to their small size, they are fiddly to do. It is worth buying extra wire and working more fingers than required. You can then select the best ones to use.

Materials
- Flesh-colored stranded cotton
- Paper-covered pieces of wire
- Embroidery scissors
- Water-based glue
- Tweezers
- Sewing thread
- Needle
- Wire cutters

Step 1

To make the fingers, you need several paper-covered pieces of wire. Using a single strand of flesh-colored stranded cotton, hold on to the wire along with the tail of the cotton and start wrapping the wire, near its center. Keep the tension so that the wraps do not unravel. Once you have worked about ¼ in/6 mm of the wire, fold the wire in half.

Step 2

Continue from where the thread is now, wrapping the two wires together. It is important to keep the tension and make sure the threads are side by side and not overlapping. Wrap for slightly longer than the length of the fingers. Then tie a knot in the thread to secure it. Add a dab of water-based glue to the knot to secure it.

Step 3

Make four fingers in the same way, and a thumb that is slightly shorter. If you made surplus fingers, select the neatest ones to use.

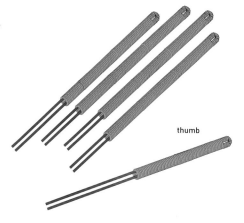

thumb

Step 4

Start to build the hand. Place all four fingers together and arrange them so that they look like a real hand. Take another length of the flesh-colored stranded cotton and start to bind the fingers together, by wrapping all four of them with the thread. Start wrapping close to the little finger, creating the palm, and go down to where the thumb will start.

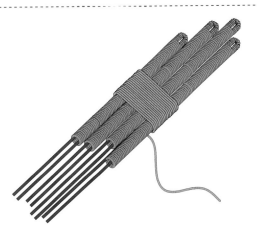

Step 5

Add in the thumb and then continue to bind the hand together. A pinch with tweezers helps to create a wrist. Continue wrapping until you have just covered where the sleeve will be. You should not be able to see the wires from under the sleeve, so go down a little further if you are unsure.

Step 6

Secure the thread with a knot and apply a small amount of glue to the knot area.

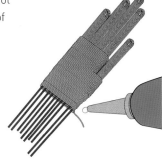

Step 7

Cut the wire a short distance from the finished wrapping.

Step 8

Apply the hand using a strong sewing thread, making sure you stitch in between the wires to secure them, catching into some of the wrapping threads. Join the hand to the arm underneath the sleeve.

NEEDLELACE

Needlelace is a lace that is produced using a needle and thread. A range of stitches create a variety of different effects. The stitches are worked in rows across a design. Needlelace can be used to make embroidered artworks and 3D jewelry.

Needlelace is a key part of the majority of stumpwork embroideries. It is believed that needlelace was developed during the Stuart period (1603–1714). At the time, the figures' outfits were made completely from needlelace. When stumpwork was at the height of its popularity during the 17th century, wealthy young ladies practiced the technique by producing complex and imaginative embroidered items, such as caskets, cushions, panels, and mirror frames.

Needlelace has many uses; the needlelace stitch you pick will depend on what you are trying to represent. Needlelace can either be worked directly onto a piece of embroidery or it can be worked on a separate frame, using a cordonnet (which is a structure for the needlelace stitches to be worked inside), and later applied to the embroidery. Needlelace uses only a thread and needle to create different patterns; these patterns have different qualities, ranging from open-lace effects to denser rows of needlelace that look like knitting.

Nowadays, the designs have evolved, and contemporary ideas for the uses of needlelace have been introduced. It can be used to create stunning clothing on contemporary stumpwork figures. Needlelace can also be worked with a wired edge (instead of the cordonnet thread), so that it can be made into three-dimensional pieces, such as brooches and jewelry. The threads in which the needlelace is worked can completely change the end result—variegated threads are very effective and allow subtle color changes.

TIP
For your first attempts, use thick threads: this makes it a lot easier to see both the pattern and any mistakes you may make.

1. Stumpwork figure with clothing worked in wired needlelace shapes on a painted background *by Masako Newton*.

Stumpwork
159

CORDONNET

— TUTORIAL —

When making a piece of needlelace that is not attached to the background embroidery, for example a piece of clothing that is going to be placed over layers of padding for the body, you need to work a cordonnet first.

Materials
- Pencil
- Tracing paper
- Muslin
- Ring frame
- Sewing thread in different colors
- Embroidery needle
- Needlelace threads
- Tapestry needle
- Tweezers
- Embroidery scissors

Step 1

Draw the needlelace shape on the tracing paper. Place the tracing paper on the muslin, in the ring frame. Stitch the tracing paper to the muslin using basting stitches. You use tracing paper because the needlelace will not be attached to the fabric.

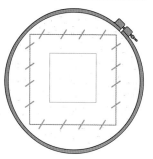

Step 2

Work a cordonnet around the shape in the same thread as the needlelace. Cut a thread long enough to wrap twice around the shape, fold it in half, and lay it in place. Work couching stitches (see page 37) over the cordonnet with an embroidery needle and sewing thread in a contrasting color, starting at the looped end.

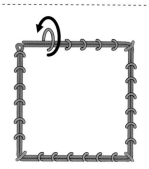

Step 3

When you get back to the looped end of the cordonnet, take the couching thread, pass it through this loop and then split it into two. Pass one of the threads back under some of the couching stitches to the left and the other to the right, then cut off the ends and finish off the couching slightly away from the shape by working two more stitches.

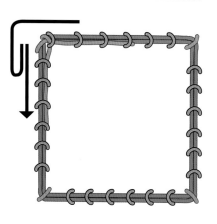

TIP
The couching stitches are temporary. Using a contrasting color makes them easier to remove later.

Step 4

Thread the tapestry needle with needlelace thread. Bring the needle up on the outside of the shape, at a corner or bend, securing with a knot. Ensure that the needlelace thread goes under the cordonnet and does not pierce the fabric. When you get to the edges, wrap the needlelace thread around the cordonnet and work back across the shape. Work the needlelace to fill the whole shape. (See pages 162–65 for needlelace stitches.)

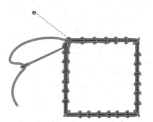

Step 5

Turn over the piece and cut away the contrasting stitches. Use tweezers to remove any remaining couching thread. Now apply the needlelace to the piece of embroidery. Work small stab stitches (see page 36) all the way around the needlelace using the tails that were left from starting and finishing the needlelace threads.

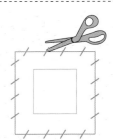

Changing the thread

If you run out of thread or wish to change color, take the thread under the cordonnet at the end of the row. Wrap it around the cordonnet three times, then secure the thread to the remaining fabric by placing a pin in the fabric and wrapping the thread around it.

Thread up the next color, and with a knot at the end, take the thread down away from the tracing paper, then bring the needle up close to where you finished off the last thread, on the outside of the shape. Wrap it twice around the cordonnet. You can now continue working the needlelace.

TIP

A cordonnet is needed only when you are working the needlelace separately and then applying it.

SINGLE BRUSSELS STITCH

—⊶— TUTORIAL —⊷—

This is the easiest needlelace stitch and forms the basic version of the other stitches. It is a buttonhole stitch that is worked in rows but the stitches are secured to the background fabric only by the edges. It is therefore important to work to a consistent tension throughout. The blue lines here represent your design lines, which can be any shape you wish.

Materials

- Fabric (any)
- Needlelace thread
- Embroidery needle
- Embroidery scissors

Step 1

Bring the needle up in the top-left corner and take it back down close to that, to form a loop. Bring the needle back up just below into the loop. You have formed one stitch. Continue working this stitch, coming out of a loop and taking the needle down on the top design line and back up in the new loop formed.

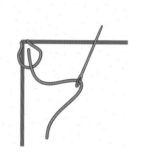

Step 2

When you get to the end, bring the needle back up just below the first row, still on the design line. Work the second row of needlelace stitches using the loop created by the first row. Bring the needle up and work the stitch into the loop, but not into the fabric, going from right to left.

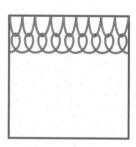

Step 3

Continue back along the shape until you get to the design line on the other side. Here, you again take the needle down through the fabric and bring it back up slightly below the previous row, ready to start the next row, which is worked through the loops of the row above and not through the fabric until you reach the other side.

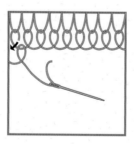

Step 4

Once you get to your final row, take the needle down into the fabric as you work each stitch, as for the first row. The needlelace will then be attached to the fabric at the top, bottom, and sides.

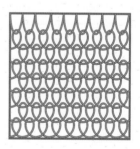

DOUBLE BRUSSELS STITCH

⊷ TUTORIAL ⊶

This is a slightly more open stitch than the single Brussels stitch so the first row of buttonhole stitches need to be slightly more spaced out. When working the second row, you work into the loops created by the first row twice—hence the name double Brussels stitch.

Materials
- Fabric (any)
- Needlelace thread
- Embroidery needle
- Embroidery scissors

Step 1

Work the first row in the same way as for the single Brussels stitch (see facing page), but make the spaces between the stitches slightly bigger.

Step 2

Take the needle down at the end of the first row and bring it back up just below. Work a needlelace stitch into the first loop of this row.

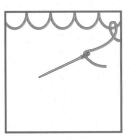

Step 3

Work a second needlelace into the same loop. Continue to work across in the same way, working two buttonhole stitches into each loop of the first row.

Step 4

Continue working back and forth across the shape, working two stitches into each loop of the previous row. On the final row, take the needle through the fabric as you work each stitch, as you did for the first row.

CORDED BUTTONHOLE STITCH

— TUTORIAL —

Corded buttonhole stitch is one of the most useful buttonhole stitches to work because it creates a dense fabric and uses a straight stitch across the shape, which helps to ensure that the tension is consistent throughout. If you find needlelace difficult, try corded buttonhole stitch first because it is slightly easier.

Materials
- Fabric (any)
- Needlelace thread
- Embroidery needle
- Embroidery scissors

Step 1

Work the first row of buttonhole stitches as on page 163. When you come back up on the design line, where you would normally work back across the shape, take the needle and thread all the way across the design to create a single stitch.

Step 2

You now have a row of buttonhole stitches and a single straight stitch below that. Bring the needle up below the single stitch and work a buttonhole stitch that goes through the loop of the first row and this single stitch.

Step 3

Continue to work a buttonhole stitch into each of the loops, incorporating the single stitch above. Each time you get to the end of a row, work another single stitch across the shape and then come up beneath that to work the next row.

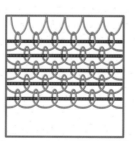

Step 4

The last row should catch into the loops and the single stitch and then go back down into the fabric. This secures the needlelace to the fabric and helps to keep the rows even.

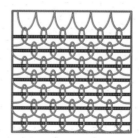

CEYLON STITCH

— TUTORIAL —

This stitch looks different from the single and double Brussels stitch, and the corded buttonhole stitches. It creates a stitch that looks similar to knitting and is therefore very useful for clothing, especially pullovers.

Materials
- Fabric (any)
- Embroidery thread
- Sewing thread
- Needlelace thread
- Embroidery needle
- Embroidery scissors

Step 1

Start by laying a single stitch of embroidery thread across the top of your design, from left to right. Secure this with a fine sewing thread in a similar color.

Step 2

Bring the needle up on the left-hand side below the single stitch of embroidery thread and work a row of loops across the line, passing the needle under the embroidery thread line, but not through the fabric, as you work each loop.

Step 3

At the end of the first row, take the needle down through the fabric and bring it back up on the left side, below the first row.

Step 4

To work the next row, pass the needle behind the loop above, without piercing the fabric. Pull the thread through to form the first loop of the second row. Continue along the row in the same way and work each subsequent row in this manner until the last row. For this row, work the stitches through the fabric to secure it.

RACHEL DOYLE
— PROFILE —

Rachel has always had a real passion and enthusiasm for crafting items by hand. At the age of eleven, she decided to focus her attention on textiles, leading her to join a textile group. This experience propelled her toward a love of embroidery. Rachel continued her studies at university where she gained a degree in textiles, after which she was accepted by the Royal School of Needlework. During her apprenticeship Rachel concentrated on perfecting her techniques, as well as developing her own style of embroidery, mainly based around small-scale intricate pieces.

- -

"I adore the miniature nature of stumpwork, as it has endless possibilities."

- -

Frequently commissioned to embroider original pieces, Rachel has also made a range of unique knitted garments in an interesting combination of knitting and embroidery.

She often takes inspiration from old family photographs and vintage embroidery finds that she gathers on her various travels. These include an array of unusual buttons and beads and are frequently integral to her personal design process. Rachel's sketchbook and camera are never far from hand, to ensure those little inspirational moments that are key to so many artists can be recorded and put to creative use. These moments often crop up in her designs and works, giving her a unique style and a truly individual portfolio.

Rachel has exhibited work in the UK and currently teaches in the UK and the USA. Her projects range from a couple of hours' work to several days of stitching. Although every piece is different, each of them feels somewhat personal: as Rachel says, "to me that is what makes hand embroidery so special."

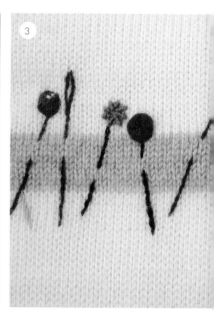

1 and 2. The bee was created as a detached slip in Turkey rug and detached wired shapes and then applied. It is worked in a range of wools and stranded cottons.
3. Close-up of machine-knitted cardigan with embroidered pins, worked in stranded cottons.
4. Three-dimensional snail, worked in a range of stranded cottons and metallic threads, grounded on a felt leaf.
5. Handmade playing cards worked in stranded cottons and metal threads on card covered in cotton.

"When using stranded cottons, separate every strand and then put them back together; this will enable the cotton to lie in a more regimented fashion."

In the future Rachel plans to continue to expand on her unique range of stumpwork pieces and further experiment with additional uses of canvas work. Rachel feels that pursuing these two techniques will open up many more avenues of possibility.

Specialty
Stumpwork and small-scale, intricate pieces

Inspired by
Vintage embroidery finds

Experiments with
Different forms of canvas work

Most challenging project
Combining knitting with embroidery

Top tip
Try using cake-decorating wire to help with fine, detailed work.

Shop
Works to commission

CHAPTER 5
WHITEWORK

Whitework refers to embroidery techniques that are traditionally worked in white threads on to a white fabric background. There are a number of different techniques, some counted and others non-counted. Traditionally, all whitework was worked in white, but as long as the technique is followed correctly, it is possible to use in different colors. However, the most effective pieces are often in traditional white.

1. Pulled work showing a range of stitches in drawn thread on evenweave fabric *by Lucy Barter*.

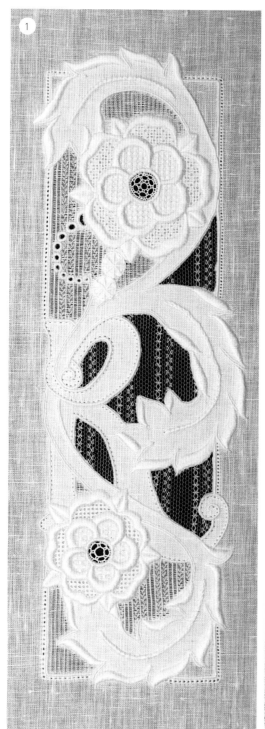

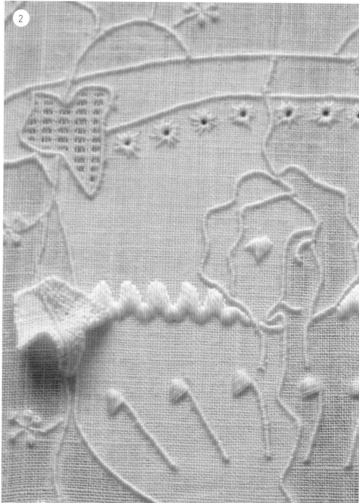

1. Fine whitework floral and monogram worked on linen *by Rebecca Ray.*
2. Fine whitework showing a range of surface stitches, pulled thread, and a wired leaf *by Margaret Dier.*
3. Close-up of a fine whitework floral and monogram design *by Rebecca Ray.*

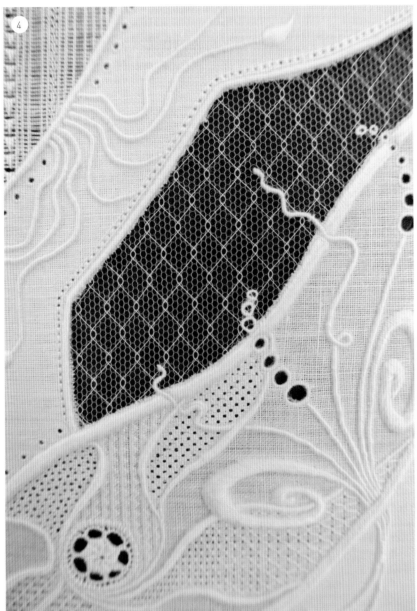

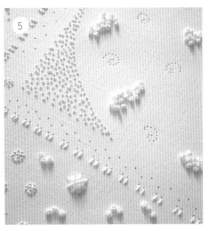

4. Fine whitework showing a combination of net darning, surface stitching such as satin stitch and eyelets, and pulled thread work *by Megumi Sorita*.
5. Paper pricking and hand embroidery worked in cotton threads onto paper *by Karen Ruane*.
6. Drawn thread worked onto white linen and made into a pin cushion *by Annick Haenni*.
7. Drawn thread work, showing a series of stages and decorative patterns, with a surfaced stitched bird *by Mary Corbet*.

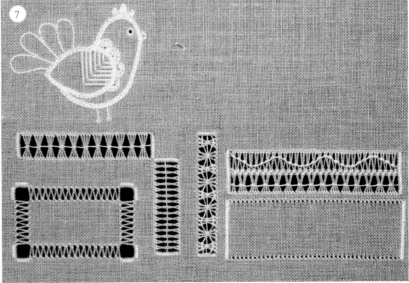

Whitework
171

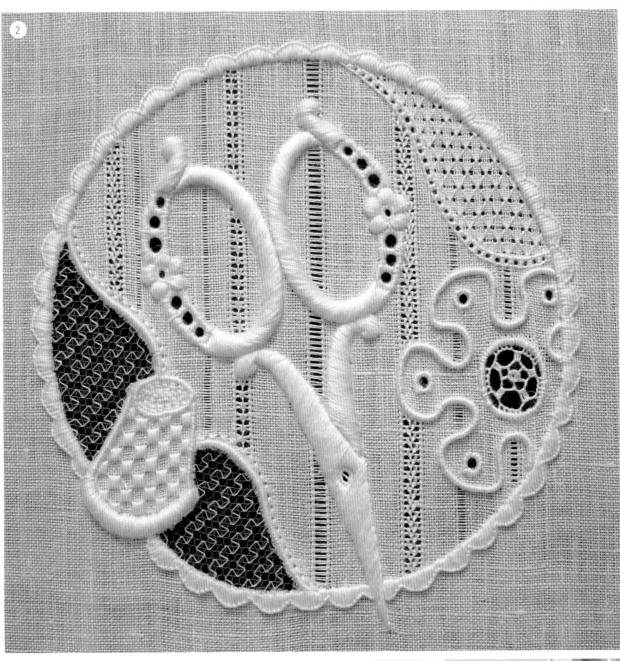

1. Fine whitework peacock worked onto linen *by Sophie Long.*
2. Fine whitework, including drawn and pulled thread, shadow appliqué, and cutwork *by Jenny Adin-Christie.*
3. Cutwork and surface stitches, including buttonhole and French knots, in stranded cotton and perle on silk dupion with a printed cotton backing *by Karen Ruane.*

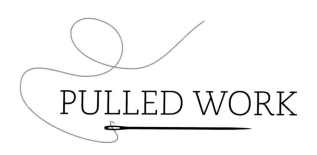

PULLED WORK

Pulled work is an ancient whitework technique that involves working stitches in extremely fine white thread on a fine cotton ground. It is often combined with other whitework techniques to produce highly delicate and detailed whitework objects, such as christening robes, petticoats, dresses, caps, handkerchiefs, tablecloths, and bed linen.

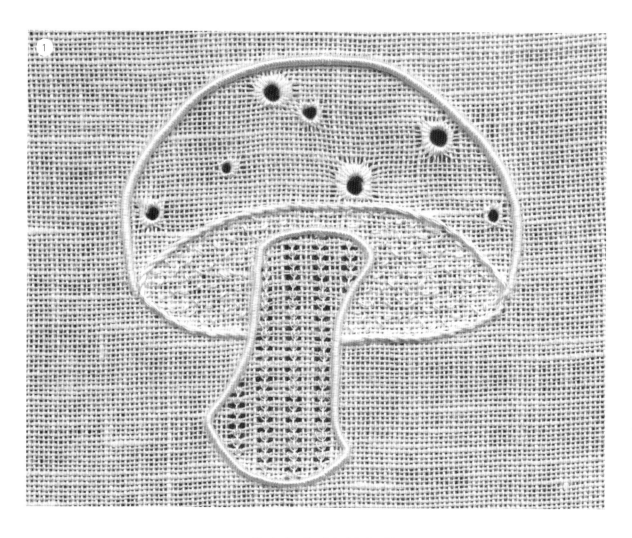

It is believed that pulled work dates back to A.D. 230–40 in India. This delicate technique was also found on a number of textiles from Germany, Egypt, and the Middle East. On these pieces, instead of white thread on a white ground fabric, colored silks and metal threads were used to work the stitches, giving a completely different look to the pieces. Therefore "pulled thread" describes the stitches used and the tension they are stitched with to create lacelike patterns, rather than the color of the "whitework."

With the industrialization of the 19th century, new threads and fabrics became widely available in Europe and the USA, including fine cambric and fine cotton, allowing embroiderers to work christening robes and delicate household items with the pulled-work technique. In other countries, embroiderers continued to work similar pulled-work stitches and patterns using the fabrics and threads available to them.

Today, a huge range of fabrics can be used for pulled work. The fabric has to be evenweave; the threads should be the same thickness so that repeat symmetrical patterns can be worked. Generally, pulled work is worked on white fabric with white threads, which produces beautiful and pure pieces of embroidery. However, there is nothing stopping today's embroiderers from working colored threads or fabrics. It is still normal for pulled work to be combined with other whitework pieces, which are generally finished and framed to keep the embroidery clean and fresh.

TIP
Work practice samples until you are confident with the technique.

HONEYCOMB 2

— TUTORIAL —

This stitch creates a series of diamond shapes and is best worked over a fairly large area so that the pattern is clearly visible. It is a fairly simple pattern to work; once you have worked the first stitch, the rest of the stitches are simply repeats.

Materials
- Linen (evenweave)
- White thread
- Tapestry needle
- Embroidery scissors

Step 1

Bring the needle up near the top right corner. Work a vertical stitch going down over four threads of the linen. Bring the needle up four threads to the left of that stitch. Take the needle down four threads above that.

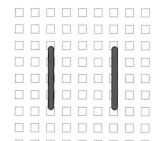

Step 2

Continue to work the four threads, working vertical stitches across the linen, with all of the horizontal stitches worked on the back.

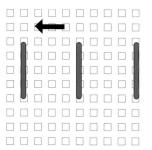

Step 3

Work the second row from the left side. Bring up the needle so that the stitches are worked as a mirror image of the first row. The straight stitch along the bottom of the first row touches the top row of the second row.

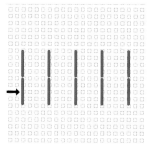

Step 4

The next row starts at the right-hand side and is worked across to the left, again as a mirror image.

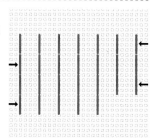

Finished effect

ROUND EYELETS 1

— TUTORIAL —

This is a circular stitch worked in rows to make a filling stitch. You can also work individual eyelets. For filling areas, it is important to count the stitches correctly. For a free style, you can work the eyelets randomly and at different sizes.

Materials

- Linen (evenweave)
- White thread
- Tapestry needle
- Embroidery scissors

Step 1

Bring the needle up at 1 and take it down at 2, going over four threads of the linen. Bring the needle back up at 3, three threads across and one down from 1. Take the needle back down to 2.

Step 2

Bring the needle up at 4 and back down into the middle of the eyelet. This is a quarter of the eyelet worked. Continue to work the same way around the middle of the eyelet until you have completed it.

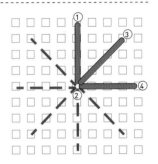

Step 3

Work the remaining eyelets in the design area in the same way. Make sure that the stitch always comes up on the outside and goes down into the middle hole, since this helps to pull the center hole larger.

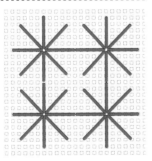

Finished effect

DIAGONAL RAISED BAND

— TUTORIAL —

This is a decorative stitch created by crosses that are worked diagonally. The tutorial explains how to work the stitch so that the diagonal is from top left to bottom right. To create it the other way, you can turn the illustrations upside down.

Materials
- Linen (evenweave)
- White thread
- Tapestry needle
- Embroidery scissors

Step 1

Starting near the bottom-right corner, work a stitch over six threads of the linen from 1 to 2. Bring the needle up three threads above and three threads to the left at 3, and take it down at 4. Continue to work in this way for subsequent stitches.

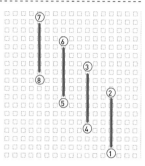

Step 2

Once you reach the top of the design, start working back down, working a horizontal line through the middle of each of the vertical stitches. After you have got the first one correctly worked, the rest should use the bottom of the previous stitch and then go into the top of the next stitch.

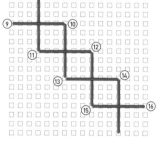

Step 3

When you reach the bottom, start the next row. Bring the needle up two threads down from the first stitch and seven threads across. Work this row in the same way as the first row—up to the top and down again.

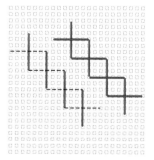

Finished effect

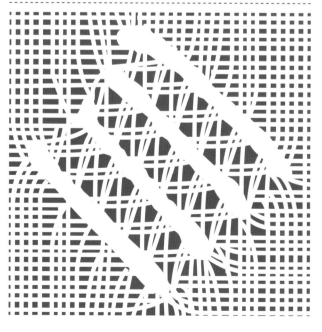

PEBBLE FILLING STITCH
— TUTORIAL —

This is a fairly simple stitch that creates circular shapes worked in rows. You can work this stitch in quite small shapes because you do not need many repeats to see the pattern.

Materials
- Linen (evenweave)
- White thread
- Tapestry needle
- Embroidery scissors

Step 1

Start this stitch toward the top right. Bring the needle up and work a stitch horizontally over three threads of the linen, then bring the needle up three threads above that and work a stitch to the left over three threads of the linen.

Step 2

Continue to work these stitches, moving between the top and bottom rows. Once you have got to the design line, work back in the other direction. Bring the needle up in the gap between the horizontal stitches, in the same hole as for the first row, and work a filling stitch. Work back across this row, filling in the gaps in the first row.

Step 3

Work the next band in the same way, from right to left, one row down from the first band, and then returning to fill the gaps.

Finished effect

BRODERIE ANGLAISE AND RICHELIEU

Broderie anglaise, or "English embroidery," is
a technique for decorating garments and household
items. It is worked by hand and machine on textiles for
the house, such as tablecloths, and for the collars and
cuffs of ladies' clothing. Like Broderie anglaise,
Richelieu work has cut areas but they are slightly
larger than the Broderie anglaise stitches.

It is not known where the technique of Broderie anglaise originates from. It was first worked in the mid-19th century and could have been developed in Scotland alongside Ayrshire work embroidery, a very delicate whitework combining surface and detailed stitches worked in open areas. Broderie anglaise became a popular technique because it could be worked on durable fabrics such as linens, and the stitches were relatively simple.

The introduction of machinery to the textile industry during the Industrial Revolution (18th and 19th centuries) made it possible to create repeat patterns using a machine. From 1870, Broderie anglaise was mass-produced.

Sewing machines today can create the stitches that are commonly used on white textiles, such as bed linen and ladies' clothing. Broderie anglaise is also still worked by hand and is often combined with Richelieu work.

Richelieu work originated in Italy in the 16th century, where it was referred to as Venetian lace. It is believed that nuns produced the earliest pieces of Richelieu work for their vestments and ecclesiastical linens. Richelieu work consists of shapes that have the fabric removed. A number of bars are worked over the shape, and buttonhole stitch is then worked to neaten the edges and strengthen the piece.

Today, Broderie anglaise is often worked on clothing; summer clothes often have eyelets as a decoration. Both Broderie anglaise and Richelieu can be combined with other whitework techniques to produce delicate embroideries. These techniques create open areas, so putting a contrasting color behind them can be very effective.

TIP
Use short threads and always wash your hands to keep the threads fresh.

ROUND EYELETS 2

— TUTORIAL —

Eyelets are small rings of stitches with the middle of the ring empty. They are very pretty when mounted with a different piece of colored fabric behind because the color is brought through. Small, round eyelets, less than ¼ in/6 mm in diameter, are made using a stiletto.

Materials
- Blue pencil
- Circle template
- White linen or cotton
- White thread
- Embroidery needle
- Embroidery scissors
- Stiletto

Step 1

With the pencil, mark onto the linen or cotton, the circles you wish to create into eyelets. To start this stitch, leave a tail of thread that will be woven in at the end. Work a small running stitch around the circle; this is the guide for working the stitches.

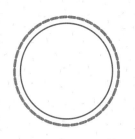

Step 2

Gently push the stiletto through the linen or cotton until it fits with the running stitches around it. The stiletto pushes the threads to the side without cutting the threads.

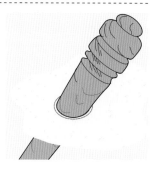

Step 3

Remove the stiletto. Bring the needle up just outside of the running stitch and take the needle down into the hole.

Step 4

Work the stitches side by side, keeping the size of the stitches the same, until you get back to the start. Weave the end threads into the back of the stitches and cut off the ends.

TIP
Use a circle template to ensure your design lines are accurate.

CUT EYELETS
— TUTORIAL —

When an eyelet is larger than ¼ in/6 mm, the threads in the middle of the eyelet need to be removed. You can then work the eyelet. Eyelets can be either circular or teardrop-shaped.

Materials
- Pencil
- White linen or cotton
- White thread
- Embroidery needle
- Embroidery scissors

Step 1

Draw the shape onto the linen or cotton. Work a running stitch around the shape.

Step 2

Pierce the inside of the shape and cut the linen or cotton vertically and horizontally, being careful not to cut the running stitches. Fold the flaps created to the back.

Step 3

Bring the needle up outside of the running stitch. Oversew from the outside of the running stitch, down into the hole, using small stitches.

Step 4

Continue to work small, even stitches around the shape.

Step 5

Once you have sewn all the way round, use a last stitch to join up the stitches. Turn the work over and trim any excess linen or cotton that has not been caught in the oversewing. Take care not to trim the oversewn stitches.

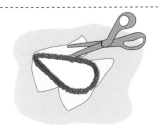

SATIN STITCH
— TUTORIAL —

You can use satin stitch for whitework, crewelwork, and appliqué. It works best over areas that are not too wide because the threads do not lie smoothly if the stitches are very long.

Materials
- White linen or cotton
- White thread
- Embroidery needle
- Embroidery scissors

Step 1

Work a split stitch from left to right, bringing the needle up at 1, then taking it down at 2 and pulling firmly. Now bring your needle up through the stitch you have just laid, piercing the thread to split it at 3, and take it down at 4.

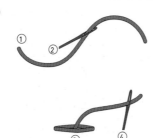

Step 2

Continue to work in this way to cover your outline.

Step 3

Bring the needle up at the top of the shape, hugging the split stitch. Make sure the needle tucks around the split stitch by angling the needle. Take it down on the other side, again hugging the split stitch. This first line of thread sets the angle for the stitching as the following stitches sit side by side next to it.

Step 4

Continue to work in this way until your shape is covered. All of the stitches should be hugging the split stitch.

BUTTONHOLE BARS
WITH OPEN AREAS
— TUTORIAL —

When making shapes that are larger than eyelets, you need to use buttonhole stitch around them; this provides a stable edge to support the cut-away area. The tight stitching of the buttonhole prevents the linen or cotton from fraying when it is cut away. However, if the cut areas are bigger than 2 in/5 cm, it is best to work bars across the shape to support them.

Materials
- Blue pencil
- White linen or cotton
- White thread
- Embroidery needle
- Embroidery scissors

Step 1

Draw the shape and work a small running stitch around it. Plan where the buttonhole bars will go. To work a bar, bring the needle up and take it straight across to the other side. Bring the needle back up that side and take it across to the first side. Ensure the stitches are taut.

Step 2

Work buttonhole stitch across the bars. Keep the tension consistent and do not pull on the bars, which will make them stretch. Finish off the thread around the outside running stitch.

Step 3

Carefully pierce the linen or cotton with your scissors, then cut it so that you can fold it back along the running-stitch line.

Step 4

Work buttonhole stitch around the main shape. Bring up the needle next to the running stitch and work the looped edge so that it is on the folded linen or cotton edge, keeping the stitches neat. oin up the start and end, then finish this thread on the back.

Step 5

Trim away any remaining linen or cotton on the back, taking care not to trim the buttonhole stitches.

DRAWN THREAD

Drawn thread is a type of counted embroidery, based on an ancient technique in which warp and weft threads are removed from a piece of evenweave fabric. The embroiderer works needle-weaving and decorative stitches in the open areas. Sometimes only the weft threads are removed, and the remaining bars are decorated or tied into bundles or groups.

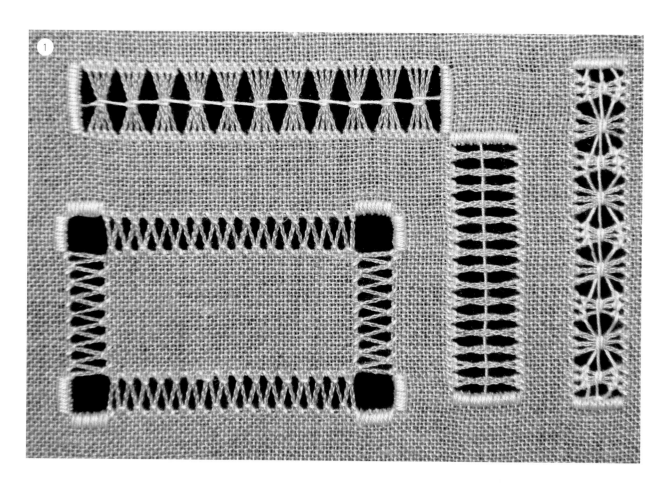

In the 15th century, drawn thread work was used on household items such as bedcovers and tablecloths. Since removing threads weakens the fabric, the drawn-thread technique was generally worked in narrow borders, often around the edge of the textiles. Other whitework techniques may have been worked alongside drawn-thread techniques, to produce textiles used for special occasions.

During the Renaissance (14th to 17th centuries), Italy was known for its delicate drawn thread work, often referred to as reticella. A pattern was worked onto the grid base formed by the threads remaining after warp and weft threads had been removed. The technique increased in popularity, spreading around Europe by the 16th century. Books were produced to help keen embroiderers to produce decorative patterns.

In the 19th and early 20th centuries, drawn thread work was often produced on linen and cotton to decorate bed and table linen. The technique was frequently combined with surface stitches such as satin stitch and crochet.

Drawn-thread work is still worked today but is not very common. It is a relatively restrictive technique because you have to remove threads to be able to work stitches into them. It is frequently combined with complementary embroidery stitches and styles, such as pulled work. The wide variety of fabric and threads available today allows the embroiderer to work at different scales, and to add beads and ribbons to the drawn-thread bars to introduce new colors and textures.

You will see some designs that have drawn thread worked so delicately that it looks like pulled work. The higher the count of linen, the smaller the drawn-thread pattern will be.

TIP
Take your time removing threads to ensure you remove the correct ones.

Whitework

REMOVING THREADS
AND REWEAVING
━━ TUTORIAL ━━

To work drawn thread, you need to remove the threads of the linen. Once you have removed the threads, you should secure them before you work any decorative stitching.

Materials
- Linen (evenweave)
- White thread
- Tacking thread
- Tapestry needle
- Embroidery scissors

Step 1

Mark out the border that you would like to work, using tacking thread. Working from the center of the border, lift up a long thread using a tapestry needle and cut it. By starting in the middle you can then gently pull that thread back both ways to the tacking thread.

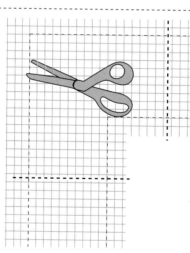

Step 2

Continue to cut the threads in the middle and pull them back to the tacking threads. Once the threads have been taken back to the tacking line, thread each one into a tapestry needle and weave it back into the linen, next to where it came from. Weave it under and over the threads, following the other end of the thread, for about four threads.

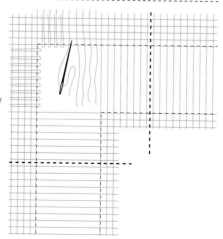

TIP
Decide what pattern you wish to work before removing any threads, because this will determine the size of the border you need.

BUTTONHOLE EDGING
— TUTORIAL —

If you have an area where you have taken in removed threads, you can use buttonhole stitch to cover up the area and make it look neater.

Materials

- Linen (evenweave)
- Thread
- Embroidery needle
- Embroidery scissors

Step 1

Secure the thread where it will not be seen. Bring the needle up on the edge to be stitched. Create a loop with the sewing thread on the front of the linen and take the needle into the linen about three threads from the edge. Bring the needle back up and through the loop, then pull firmly. Continue to work buttonhole stitches, with no gaps between them, so the edge is secure.

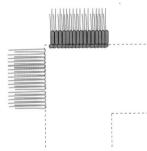

Step 2

Work up to the corner and then turn the corner at a right angle and continue down the other side. Both sides have a buttonhole edge, to create an L shape.

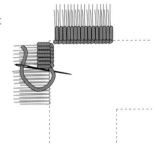

Step 3

Finish off the buttonhole stitches. Then remove the rewoven threads of the linen, by pulling on the threads tightly while cutting them off. The tension should cause the threads to fall back into the buttonhole stitch.

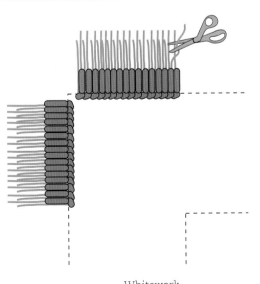

TIP

With all whitework, it is important that the thread is as clean as possible. If the thread is starting to look worn, it is best to change it.

HEM STITCH

—◯— TUTORIAL —◯—

Work hem stitch to secure a border, add strength, and to gather remaining threads so that you can work a pattern. You work the hem stitch in the border of the open area, slightly into the surrounding linen, wrapping around the start of the threads that remain in the open area.

Materials
- Linen (evenweave) with bar threads removed
- White thread
- Tapestry needle
- Embroidery scissors

Step 1

Hem stitch is worked from right to left, using a tapestry needle. Secure the thread and bring the needle up from behind, three threads along. Thread the needle back around the group of threads and up again from the same place, pulling the threads together.

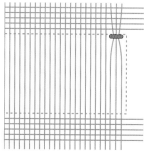

Step 2

Take the needle into the linen vertically over two threads.

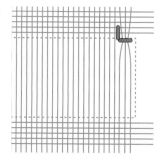

Step 3

Bring the needle up a further three threads along, ready to start the next stitch.

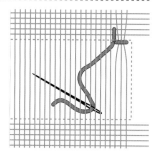

Step 4

Continue to work hem stitch all the way along the bar. Work the same stitch on the opposite side. Make sure that the stitches match up so that the threads are gathered symmetrically on both sides.

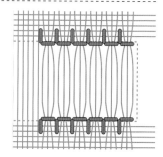

TIP
You can add decorative stitches to the threads of fabric you are left with.

KNOTTING BORDER
— TUTORIAL —

A knotting border is a way of gathering threads in the open bar. It involves working a thread along the middle of the bar, and wrapping it around the threads that remain in that bar.

Materials
- Linen (evenweave) with bar threads removed
- White thread
- Tapestry needle
- Embroidery scissors

Step 1

Work this stitch from right to left, using a tapestry needle. Secure the thread in the middle of the edge of the bar. The thread needs to be long enough to reach the whole way across the bar since you will not be able to secure a thread and start a new one.

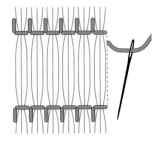

Step 2

Loop the needle under three groups of threads and back over the same three groups of threads.

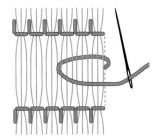

Step 3

Take the needle down through the loop of the sewing thread ...

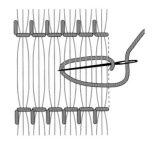

Step 4

... and pull it through to form a knot that lies on top of the threads.

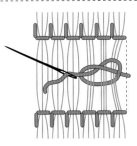

Step 5

Work the next stitch in the same way. Continue to work the knots all the way across the bar.

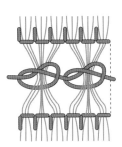

WOVEN WHEEL CORNER
—— TUTORIAL ——

This is a woven wheel, similar to the technique used in ribbon work (page 129). You can work it clockwise or anticlockwise, over an odd number of spokes.

Materials
- Linen (evenweave) with buttonhole around the corner
- White thread
- Tapestry needle
- Embroidery scissors

Step 1

Work the spokes first. The first one goes from the middle of the square from 1 to 2. Bring the needle up at 1 and wrap the thread around the spoke until you get to the middle. Then take the thread across to 2 and work back to the middle. Always work the spoke opposite to maintain even tension in the square.

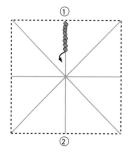

Step 2

Take the needle down in the center and bring it up at 3. Wrap it around the spoke back to the middle. Do the same to work from 4 back. Wrap from 6 to 5 in the same way. As woven wheels have to be worked over an odd number of spokes, when you get to 7, stop. Spoke 8 is worked at a later stage.

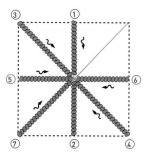

Step 3

Bring the thread back to the middle, winding around the spoke. Work a loop knot over the spokes to gather them all up, take the needle behind all of the spokes, and pull it up.

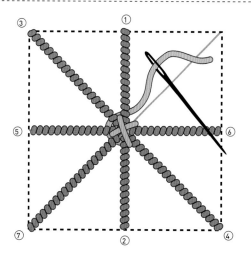

Step 4

Use the thread to weave around the wheel, taking the thread under and over the spokes until you get to the size of wheel that you want. Continue to weave until you get to 1.

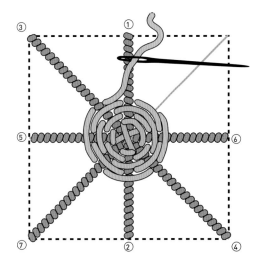

Step 5

Bring up the thread from one of the weaves of the web and use it to wind around spoke 8, down to the woven wheel. Wind the thread around spoke 1. Now all of the spokes are wrapped, and you have a wheel in the middle. Finish off the remaining thread.

TIP

If you are unsure about the tension you need for the spokes, work a practice corner first; too tight and it will pull the corner, too loose and the spokes will not be supported.

JENNY ADIN-CHRISTIE
PROFILE

Jenny's whitework is hugely inspired by the work of Lady Evelyn Stewart Murray (1868–1940), of Perthshire, Scotland. She was a great admirer of fine whitework, and created a fabulous collection of exquisite examples. Jenny also takes inspiration from the intricate creations of the 19th-century Scottish workers of Ayrshire embroidery. The baby gowns of this period show whitework reaching a peak of artistry and design.

Jenny likes to employ the full range of traditional whitework techniques in her work. This provides her with a huge palette of stitches, which she thinks of as a "whitework tonal scale," running from the "whitest" stitches: those that add density and whiteness to the ground fabric (such as shadow appliqué, padded satin stitch, counted satin stitches, long and short stitch, and trailing); through those that eat into the fabric, opening up the surface and allowing light to permeate (such as pulled and drawn work stitches); and finally those that allow sections of fabric to be taken away, revealing what lies beneath (such as eyelets, ladder stitch, and needlerun net insertion).

> "I am endlessly fascinated by the pattern forms and architectural structures to be found in the natural world, and in contrast by the intricate pattern forms of buildings and wrought iron."

She uses fine-quality fabrics, generally Italian or Belgian linen batistes, together with English tulle. Her threads are basic white embroidery threads, such as stranded cotton, cotton perles, coton a broder, Retors D'Alsace, floche a broder, and a selection of fine cotton lace threads.

Jenny principally works embroideries to individual commission. She has displayed her whitework at specialist exhibitions in many locations and exhibits her work at Embroiderers' Guild and similar group events in countries, including the UK, Ireland, and Australia.

1. A combination of net darning, satin stitch, trailing, and eyelets finished with a buttonhole scalloped edge, worked on silk organza and conservation net.
2. Whitework sampler, including a drawn-thread band at the bottom, eyelets, and buttonhole bars worked on linen, stitched using stranded cottons and flower thread.

3. A range of hand embroidered whitework buttons, worked in a range of whitework techniques on linen and organza fabrics.
4. A fine whitework piece, including surface stitches, appliqué, drawn and pulled thread, and cutwork worked onto fine linen with conservation net inserted.

"If you would like to practice whitework, attend a specialist workshop and learn how to handle the stitches expertly. Whitework does not read well if the stitches are not well executed."

Specialty
Individually commissioned whitework pieces

Inspired by
Intricate 19th-century whitework

Experiments with
Density of stitches and techniques within whitework

Most challenging process
Learning to work at speed

Top tip
The way your needle is placed and taken through the fabric governs how the thread will lie, so learn to manipulate the needle adeptly.

Shop
Works to commission

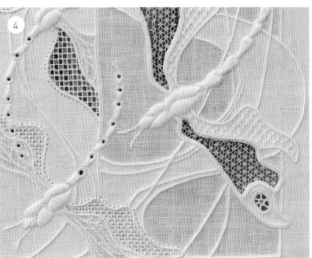

CHAPTER 6

THREE-DIMENSIONAL EMBROIDERY

Three-dimensional embroidery makes objects rather
than flat embroideries. Smocking and hand quilting are
ways of using fabrics to create textured pieces of art,
home furnishings, and clothing. Box and tassel making
are techniques for creating objects using fabric and
threads. These techniques are all created by hand.
Learning them will expand your knowledge of the
specific technique and provide you with skills that can
be combined with other embroidery techniques.

1. Hand quilted using perle embroidery thread *by Rita Hodge.*

Three-Dimensional Embroidery

1. Appliqué and hand quilting using cotton threads on assorted cotton fabrics *by Victoria Gertenbach.*
2. Hand-smocked polka-dot cotton pleated bag *by Esther Sanchez and Estella Straatsma.*
3. Machine quilted onto cotton with polyester threads *by Fabienne Chabrolin.*
4. Embroidered cotton pieces sewn together into a crazy patchwork cushion *by Royal School of Needlework staff.*

Three-Dimensional Embroidery

1. Hand quilted using perle embroidery thread *by Rita Hodge*.

2 and 3. Machine quilted with surface embroidery and trapunto on white cotton *by Emma How*.

4. Handmade box, covered in printed quilting fabric; box top embroidered with appliqué and surface stitches using silk ribbons and stranded cottons *by Zinaida Kazban*.

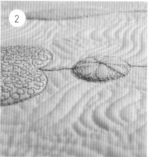

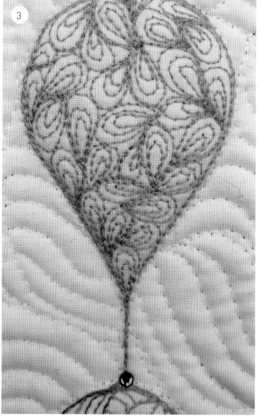

5. Diamond-smocked doll's dress worked on cotton using stranded cotton and beads *by Susan Bischoff.*
6. Handmade tassel made with a range of wools and embellished with wool pompoms *by Grace Walsh.*
7. Hand-smocked honeycomb purse worked on Alcantara fabric *by Esther Sanchez and Estella Straatsma.*

SMOCKING

Smocking is used to control the fullness of the fabric by creating pleats secured with embroidery stitches. Nowadays, it is used as a decorative art in its own right. By stitching the fabric in repeat patterns, interesting textures can be created, to be used alone or as a surface for embroidery.

1. Handsmocked baby's dress embroidered with stranded cottons *by Kathi Alderink* (photo by MRD photography).
2. Smocking using a variety of threads on silk *by Lucy Margolius.*
3. Smocked gingham bag *by Esther Sanchez and Estella Straatsma.*

Smocking began in England around the 13th or 14th century, and up until the 19th century it was used on practical outer garments worn by farm workers and laborers. Although made and embroidered by women, these garments were almost exclusively worn by men and were often embroidered with symbols relating to their occupations. Smocks were made in a heavy linen fabric, parts of which were gathered into pleats and then secured with embroidery stitches. These garments provided warmth from the winter weather and their loose construction gave freedom of movement to the wearer.

In the 19th century, agriculture was mechanized, and loose garments became hazardous to wear while operating machinery. Consequently, the wearing of the rural smock gradually died out, although smocking started to gain popularity for use on women's and children's clothing. In the mid-19th century, smocking became a popular decorative art form on the garments of upper-class women, and in the latter half of the century it became fashionable for children's outfits, with patterns for smocking embroideries appearing in magazines. The use of smocking on garments spread to Europe and later to the USA, Australia, and New Zealand. By the early 20th century, this style of decorating garments was extremely fashionable.

In the 1940s a smocking pleating machine was invented; this revolutionized the art by eliminating the laborious process of hand pleating the fabric prior to applying the embroidery stitches. Smocking has gone in and out of fashion for ladieswear over the years and today is mostly seen on babies' and children's clothing. It is also used creatively to make cushions and other home accessories, using unconventional stitches and contemporary designs.

3

2

SEAMLESS TUCKS: PUFFS

— TUTORIAL —

This type of smocking creates round, raised areas of fabric, which are in rows. The puffs are formed by stitching individual stitches by hand on the back of the fabric.

Materials
- Smocking dots
- Pen or pencil
- Light box
- Fabric (any)
- Sewing thread in a matching color
- Embroidery needle
- Embroidery scissors

Step 1

Mark a grid on the back of the fabric using smocking dots. You can trace it using a pen or pencil but test it out before you start. The dots should be discreet so that they are not visible once you finish. You may need a light box behind the dots so that you can see them through the fabric. Otherwise, tape the dots to a window and use sunlight to help you trace them on.

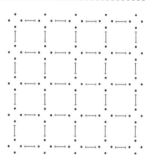

Step 2

With a length of sewing thread in the needle, take the needle down on a dot on the back of the fabric and bring it back up at the next dot, leaving a tail. Repeat this stitch, taking the needle down and up at the same dots.

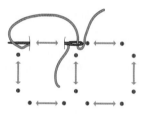

Step 3

Pull the thread to draw the dots together. Secure the needle and tail ends of the thread with a square knot. Wrap the right end over the left, then the left over the right to form a loop as shown. Pull the four ends to draw the loop tight. Cut off, leaving a small amount of thread. Continue working stitches and knots in horizontal rows, pushing the puffs to the front of the fabric once gathered.

Finished effect

NORTH AMERICAN SMOCKING: LOZENGE

— TUTORIAL —

This type of smocking creates rectangular raised bars that are created by working small stitches that are pulled tight and slack stitches joining the raised bars.

Materials
- Smocking dots
- Pen or pencil
- Light box
- Fabric (any)
- Sewing thread in a matching color
- Embroidery needle
- Embroidery scissors

Step 1

For this type of smocking, smocking dots are required. You can buy them or create your own, using graph paper. Trace the dots on to the front of the fabric (see facing page). Use a pen or pencil, depending on the fabric. You may need to use a light box if your fabric is dark.

Step 2

Starting with a knot on the end of the sewing thread, bring the needle up at the back of the fabric at dot 1. Pick up dot number 2 and work back to 1. Pull the thread tightly so that the dots are together.

Step 3

Travel along the back, leaving a slack thread. Bring the needle up at 3 and tie a knot to ensure that the thread remains slack. Pick up dot 4 and return to pick up dot 3, pulling these dots together. Pick up dot 5 and tie another knot. Continue to work across the fabric, gathering the dots and tying knots to leave a slack thread.

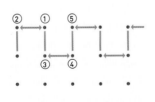

Finished effect

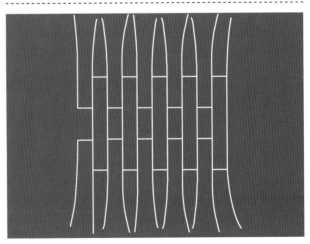

NORTH AMERICAN
SMOCKING: FLOWER
——◦— TUTORIAL —◦——

This type of smocking creates flower shapes by working small stitches that gather the fabric, followed by a slack stitch that links to the next small gathering stitch.

Materials
- Smocking dots
- Pen or pencil
- Light box
- Fabric (any)
- Sewing thread in a matching color
- Embroidery needle
- Embroidery scissors

Step 1

For this type of smocking, smocking dots are required. You can buy them or create your own, using graph paper. Trace the dots on to the front of the fabric (see page 204). Use a pen or pencil, depending on the fabric.

Step 2

Thread up some sewing thread and put a knot on the back of the fabric. Bring the needle up at 1, pick up dots 2, 3, and 4, and then go back to 1, using small stitches with the needle angled into the middle of the square.

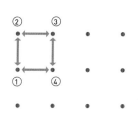

Step 3

Pull up the thread, so that the dots are pulled together. Work a small invisible stitch to secure this flower. Take the thread along to the next flower, ensuring that it remains slack. Bring the needle along and up at 5. Repeat the last step by picking up dots 6, 7, and 8 and going back to 5. Pull up the thread so that the dots are together and again work a small securing stitch. Repeat, working across the fabric in horizontal rows. When you have finished stitching, manipulate the flowers to raise all the petals.

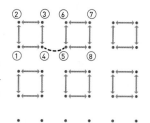

Finished effect

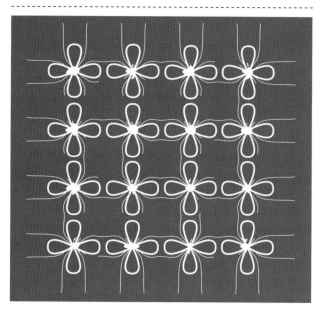

NORTH AMERICAN
SMOCKING: LATTICE

━━━━◯─── TUTORIAL ━━◯━━

This type of smocking creates a lattice by working small stitches diagonally to gather the fabric. You work in rows down the fabric, jumping from left to right.

Materials
- Smocking dots
- Pen or pencil
- Light box
- Fabric (any)
- Sewing thread in a matching color
- Embroidery needle
- Embroidery scissors

Step 1

For this type of smocking, smocking dots are required. You can buy them or create your own, using graph paper. Trace the dots on to the front of the fabric (see page 204), using a pen or pencil, depending on the fabric. You may need to use a light box if your fabric is dark.

Step 2

Start with the knot on the back of the fabric. Bring the needle up at dot 1 and pick up 2, then return to dot 1. Pull up the thread so that these dots are gathered together.

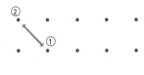

Step 3

Travel along the back and pick up dot 3. Tie a knot to keep the threads slack. Pick up dot 4 and then return to dot 3. Pull them together tightly. Continue working these steps in vertical rows across the fabric, gathering the dots, leaving a slack thread, and tying knots.

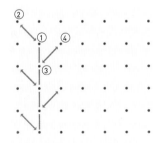

Finished effect

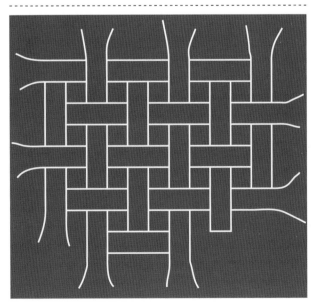

SMOCKING PLEATER

— TUTORIAL —

You can use a smocking pleater to pleat the fabric ready for working surface stitches onto it. The machine consists of cogs that turn a row of needles to stitch through the pleats. Remember that the fabric will be greatly reduced once it is pleated, so allow three or four times the amount that you need at the end.

Materials
- Smocking machine
- Smocking machine needles
- Fabric (any)
- Sewing thread to match fabric
- Embroidery scissors
- Fabric scissors

Step 1

Thread each of the needles in the machine with a length of double sewing thread, which should be about 4 in/10 cm longer than the length of the fabric.

Step 2

Roll the fabric around the dowel at the back of the pleater; ensure that the selvedge has been removed. Make sure that the grain of the fabric is straight where it feeds into the pleater.

Step 3

Feed the fabric into the pleater. Turn the knob so that the cogs move the fabric on to the needles.

Step 4

Gently push the pleats on to the thread. The fabric will pleat around the needles. Continue to do this, gently pushing down the pleated fabric on to the threads.

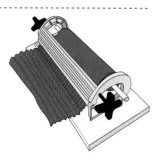

Step 5

Once all of the fabric has been worked, cut the threads close to the needles, to remove the pleated fabric.

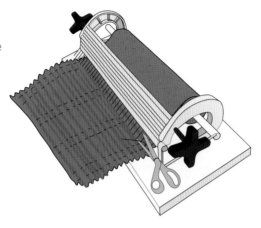

Step 6

Ensure that the pleats are evenly spaced; you need to be able to see the gathering threads between each gather. Finish off the loose ends and tie them in pairs so that the threads cannot be pulled through the pleats.

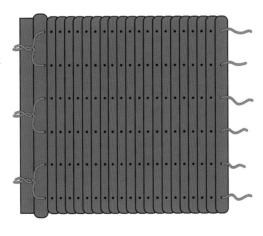

TIP

If you do not have a smocking pleater, you can pleat by hand. Gingham is a good fabric to practice on because you can use the pattern as a grid.

SMOCKING PLEATER STITCHES
⊶ TUTORIAL ⊷

Once you have made pleats (see page 208), you can work stitches onto the pleated fabric. Plan your work first; you should work the stitches across the pleats, using the folds to keep the stitches consistent. Use stranded cottons in a range of colors to work the stitches.

Materials
- Pleated fabric (any)
- Embroidery needle
- Stranded cottons in a range of colors
- Embroidery scissors

HONEYCOMB

Step 1

Bring the needle up on the left of the first pleat and over the first two pleats. Stitch into the right-hand side of the second pleat and back through to the first pleat.

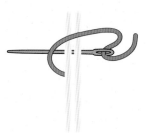

Step 2

Repeat to make a second stitch just below the first, and pull the fabric folds gently together.

Step 3

Move down to begin your second row of stitches. Bring the needle up on the left of the second pleat, over the second and third pleats, stitch into the right-hand side of the third pleat and back through the second pleat. Repeat to make another stitch below this.

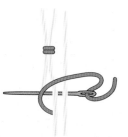

Step 4

Go back to the top row and repeat this process all the way along the fabric, moving up and down the pleats for every alternate row. Move down and repeat for two rows below this, and so on, until the stitching is complete.

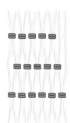

CABLE

Step 1

Bring the needle up on the left of the first pleat, over to the right-hand side of the second pleat, then back up between the first and second pleats.

Step 2

Take the needle over to the right-hand side of the third pleat, then back up between the second and third pleats. This forms a stitch sitting next to, and just above, the first.

Step 3

Continue working in this way along the fabric, with every even stitch sitting above every odd stitch.

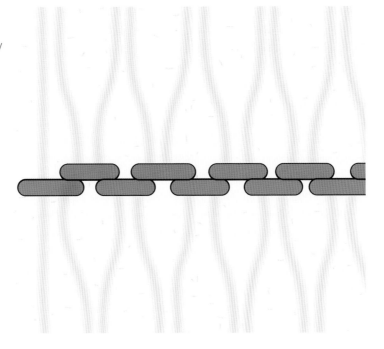

WAVE AND TRELLIS

Step 1

Tack a line across the top the area you wish to fill with wave and trellis stitch. Bring the needle up at this line, on the left-hand side of the first pleat, take it back through the second pleat, and up between the two.

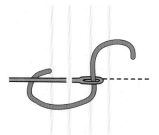

Step 2

Take the needle over and back through the third pleat, bringing it up again between the second and third pleats. Continue to work stitches down the fabric in the same way, pleat by pleat.

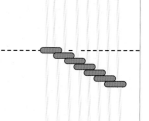

Step 3

Once you reach the gathering thread, start to work the stitches up again, back to the original tacking line. Work them back down. Continue in this way across the whole of the fabric.

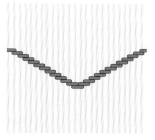

Step 4

Go back to the left-hand side of the first pleat, below your first stitching line, and follow the same process, but working upward and downward in reverse.

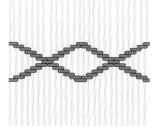

1. Close-up of smocked pleated bag worked onto wool gingham *by Esther Sanchez and Estella Straatsma.*

Three-Dimensional Embroidery

EMBROIDERED BOXES

Embroidered boxes can be worked in a range
of different shapes and sizes, using any embroidery
technique. Each side of the box is cut out and covered
with fabric, and then the parts are sewn together.
Box making requires accuracy and precision
to ensure that the parts fit together neatly.

Small embroidered boxes or caskets can be traced back to the Middle Ages (5th to 15th centuries), when they were used to keep the bones and various relics of saints. These boxes were known as reliquaries and were vital assets in churches and abbeys for the focus of prayer.

During the mid-17th century in England and Europe, embroidered boxes with the unique style of three-dimensional stumpwork or raised work became fashionable and were often luxuriously embellished with pictures. These boxes were called caskets; each side was embroidered as well as the drawers, doors, and lids. Caskets were generally stitched by young girls who were learning embroidery. The caskets had a series of compartments for storing jewelry, writing equipment, letters, and needlework tools. They often had one or two secret drawers for the safekeeping of their young owners' most precious possessions. The young women stitched the embroideries, and the pieces of fabric, which were then given to a cabinet maker to make up the box.

Nowadays, it is most common to make the box up yourself rather than sending it to a cabinet maker. The project has to be well planned so that both the measurements and the embroidery are perfect. Making an embroidery box is a real skill, but the possibilities are endless.

The boxes made today are often fun and creative. They are sometimes square with beautiful embroidery, or in the shape of an object, such as a treasure chest, with a curved lid.

②

TIP

Start by working a small, simple box. Once you understand the process, you can design more detailed ones.

Three-Dimensional Embroidery

BOX-MAKING PRIMER

Fabric-covered boxes are a real test of your accuracy. Each piece of card is cut out by hand and covered in fabric; these are then sewn together by hand. You make the outside and inside of the box so that each piece of card has a matching piece, which you put together to form the exterior and interior. If you would like embroidery on the box, plan it during the design stage and work it on a frame to ensure that the tension is tight so that it will be tight around the pieces of card when made in to the box. First, make a mock-up box using thin card to work out the size and construction.

DRAWERS

If you wish to include drawers in your box, include them in the mock-up version. A drawer is basically another small box, without a lid. It is made in the same way, by covering the card and then sewing the parts together. As for the boxes, you need to make interior and exterior pieces of card because the outside as well as the inside of the drawer will be visible.

It is important for drawers to move smoothly. When working out the measurements, allow an extra ⅛ in/3 mm so that the drawer slides easily. Using a smooth material for the drawer will help.

When designing, consider whether you would like the drawer to come completely out of the box, or whether you would prefer it to be secured so that once you have pulled it partly out, it cannot be pulled fully out. If you wish it to be restricted, attach a piece of ribbon to the back of the drawer and the inside of the box to limit how far it can be pulled out.

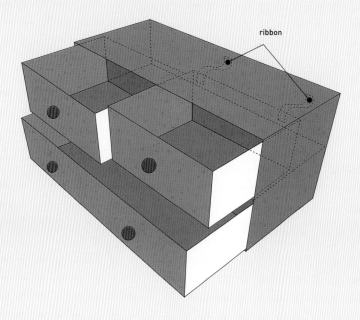

ribbon

MEASURING AND CUTTING

Once you have designed your box and made a mock-up version, you are ready to measure and cut out the pieces, and pad the internal pieces of card. The measurements listed at right will make a box that is 2 in/5 cm cubed.

Draw each piece using a pencil and ruler and check it with a set square before and after cutting the card. Allow ⅛ in/3 mm for the thickness of the card and the fabric around it. If you are using a material thicker than cotton, you may need to allow more than ⅛ in/3 mm.

Cut out all the parts of the box, labeling each piece of card as you cut.

PADDING

If you want to pad the internal pieces of card, use a layer of felt; the color of the felt you use should match the material used over the top. The felt should be cut approximately ⅛ in/3 mm smaller than the card to allow for the over-lapping of the pieces of card once it is put together. Apply the felt to the card with double-sided tape. You can also pad the top of the box if you wish.

External measurements

Note that the external top and bottom of the box are on the outside. The front and back sit inside of the top and bottom, as do the sides.

Top and bottom 2 × 2 in/5 × 5 cm
Front and back 2 × 1¹³⁄₁₆ in/5 × 4.6 cm
Sides 1¹³⁄₁₆ × 1¹³⁄₁₆ in/4.6 × 4.6 cm

Internal measurements

Top 1¹¹⁄₁₆ × 1¹⁰⁄₁₆ in/4.2 × 4.2 cm
Bottom 1¹³⁄₁₆ × 1¹³⁄₁₆ in/4.6 × 4.6 cm
Front 1¹³⁄₁₆ × 1¹¹⁄₁₆ in/4.6 × 4.4 cm
Back 1¹³⁄₁₆ × 1¹¹⁄₁₆ in/4.6 × 4.4 cm
Sides 1¹⁰⁄₁₆ × 1¹¹⁄₁₆ in/4.2 × 4.4 cm

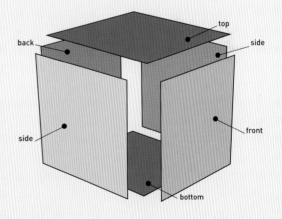

COVERING THE CARD
━ TUTORIAL ━

Once you have padded the interior of the box, you can cover the pieces of card with fabric. A plain cotton or one with a small print works well for this size of box.

Materials
- Cardboard
- Fabric (any)
- Felt
- Double-sided tape
- Needle
- Thread
- Fabric and embroidery scissors

Step 1

Place each external piece of card on to the fabric and cut the fabric ½ in/13 mm bigger all the way around the card. Make sure that the fabric is straight on the grain so that once the card is covered it will remain so.

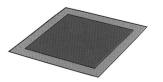

Step 2

For the internal pieces, place the card felt down on the fabric. Place two pieces of double-sided tape down the sides of the card. Remove the protective tape, and bring the fabric around to the back. Pull it as taut as possible, checking that it is on the grain.

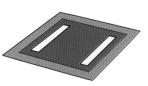

Step 3

Fold in the corners, or trim them off to remove some fabric bulk. Attach the other two sides using the double-sided tape. Cover all of the pieces of card in this same way except for the external lid.

Step 4

Lace the external lid. Place the card on the fabric, on the grain. Fold in a corner to make a miter. With matching sewing thread, work a slip stitch. Take a small stitch from one side of the fold, and go to the other side; take a small stitch. Repeat for all corners.

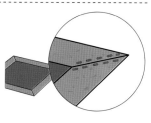

Step 5

Once all corners are secure, lace the back of the lid, using a long thread. Work stitches backward and forward across the card. Make sure that the lacing is not too close to the edge. Finish off the thread once it is taut, and the fabric is smooth and on the grain.

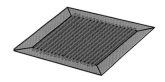

LIDS

— TUTORIAL —

Depending on the style of box you want to make, there are a number of different possibilities for making lids. For the square box in the tutorial in this chapter (see page 220), the lid is similar to the box sides. The box lid can be joined to the box using the slip-stitch method on the opposite page or can be a separate part. You can create the square box with a separate lid by not slip stitching down the hinge side; this way, the lid sits on top of the box.

Materials
- Exterior and interior box
- Card
- Cutting knife and board
- Fabric (any)
- Curved needle
- Thread to match fabric
- Double-sided tape
- Ruler and pencil

Step 1

To create a box that is similar to a shoe box, make two boxes with four sides and a base: the main box and the lid. The main box is the bottom box; make this to the size you wish the box to be.

Step 2

Construct the lid box. It should sit on the outside of the box, so the measurements should reflect this. The depth of the lid depends on the design.

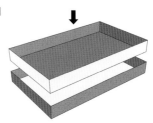

Step 3

Sew the lid together with slip stitch as described on page 220. Once you have created both boxes, the lid sits on the main box.

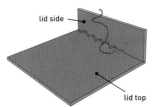

lid side

lid top

TIP

Remember that the top few inches of the main box (depending on the design) will be covered by the lid, so when planning embroidery or embellishments for the box, leave this section free. Note that embroidery or embellishments will add bulk and may prevent the lid from fitting properly.

CONSTRUCTION OF THE BOX

— TUTORIAL —

The internal and external boxes are assembled separately. Put the external pieces and the lids to one side, and put together the internal box first. Remember that the front and back of the box are the full size, so the side pieces should fit in between them.

Materials
- Fabric-covered pieces of card
- Sewing thread to match fabric
- Curved needle
- Embroidery scissors
- Glass-headed pins

Step 1

Using a length of sewing thread in a matching color to the fabric and a small curved needle, stitch the bottom piece of the internal box to the front piece. Use a slip stitch and work tiny stitches, which should be invisible.

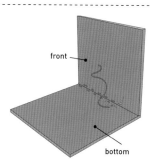

Step 2

Attach the remaining pieces in the same way.

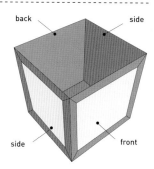

Step 3

Now put together the external box in the same way. Gently slip the internal box inside the external box; it should fit snugly. Work a slip stitch around the top of the box, joining the internal and external pieces of card.

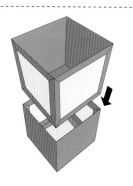

Step 4

Place the internal lid on to the external lid. Pin it in place so that it is central. Slip stitch around the two pieces to complete the lid.

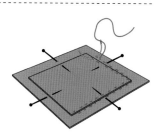

Step 5

Secure the lid in the same way as the other pieces. Use a slip stitch along one side of the lid and the box. This works as a hinge for the box.

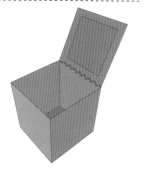

TIP

Plain fabric is slightly easier to work with than patterned fabric; patterned fabrics can look messy if they do not line up around the box.

1. Handmade cake box, covered using cotton and printed cottons *by Maki Saeki*.

Three-Dimensional Embroidery

TASSEL MAKING

A tassel is a dangling ornament made with a range of threads of even length laid parallel together and fastened at one end. Tassels can be as plain or as decorative as you like. Making tassels for home furnishings is a great way to liven up a room and to pull together a range of textures and colors. They are a good way to use up spare threads and beads too.

1

Tassels were used by weavers to knot the loose ends of yarn together on the edges of blankets, rugs, and clothing. During the 14th century, tassels were used on uniforms in Europe as a symbol of wealth and status that differentiated people in military, religious, and academic fields. They have been used on decorative furnishings such as cushions, curtains, and furniture since the 15th century.

Tassels gradually became more complex and decorative, reaching a pinnacle of elegance during the 17th century, especially in France, where skilled artisans used costly silks and metallic threads to produce them. By the 19th century, tassels were used to trim everything from horses, carriages, cushions, and curtain tie-backs, to keys.

In India, it is traditional to use a range of sophisticated textile items, such as tassels, embroideries, and fringing, as adornments for bridal dresses and temple furnishings.

Tassel making is a fairly slow process because you need to make several elements—the cord, ruffs, head, and skirt—but the techniques are relatively easy. The range of tassel molds and threads available today means the possibilities are endless.

TIP
Only use threads that can be put under a lot of tension without snapping. Stranded cottons and crewel wools work well.

It is best to make a design of the tassel before you start. Think about which threads you will use for the:

- skirt
- ruffs
- cords for the tassel heads
- cords for the suspension
- embellishments for the skirt

Three-Dimensional Embroidery

CORD

TUTORIAL

Cords are widely used in embroidery, for example, to cover the edge when applying fabric. On tassels, cords are used to cover the wooden head. You can make cords with two, three, or four strands, depending on the design. The strands could all be different, making a stripy cord, or they could all have the same thread combination.

Materials
- Threads
- Cord maker
- G clamps
- Knitting needles
- Strong sewing thread
- Embroidery needle
- Embroidery scissors

Step 1

Attach the clamp and hooks onto a table. Attach the thread combinations to them and then to the cord-maker's hooks. Make sure that the threads do not cross over. Trim off small pieces of loose thread close to the hooks.

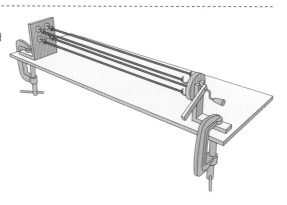

Step 2

Holding the cord-maker's drum with your thumb, turn the handle using the other hand. The threads should twist together, but still be separate and not crossed over. Ask a friend to check that they are not tangling up. Continue twisting the threads. To check whether you have twisted them enough, stop turning and test one of the thread combinations by gently pulling on the thread; it should spring slightly into a knot. If this happens, move on to the next step; if not, carry on turning.

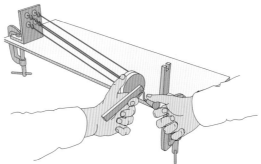

TIP
Note that when threads are spun into a cord, you lose some of the length. It is best to add one-third extra length. If in doubt, make a cord longer than you need.

Step 3

Remove your thumb from the drum and continue to turn the handle. You should see the cord forming. At this stage, it is best to ask a friend to help to guide the thread combinations to ensure that there are no "jumps." Ask the friend to put knitting needles between the thread combinations to make sure that the correct sequence is created.

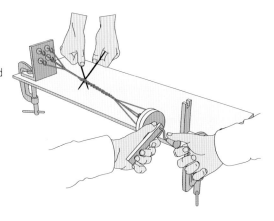

Step 4

Once the cord has been spun all of the way, ask your friend to hold on to the cord maker and thread up some strong sewing thread. Finish off both ends of the cord, taking the needle through the cord, and then bind it. Make sure it is completely secure. Start to gently release the cord from the cord maker, working along the cord.

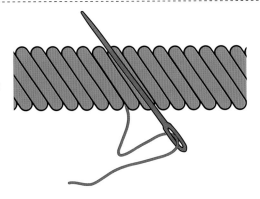

Suspension cord

The tassel is hung with a thick suspension cord. For this, you need to make two separate cords about four times the desired length of the rope. Bind the ends of both of the cords. Attach them to the cord maker, folding both of the cords in half. Twist the cords together with the cord maker, using knitting needles to ensure that the pattern is consistent along the rope. Bind the ends to secure them.

TIP
Cord makers vary slightly. Check the instructions on yours before you start.

HEAD

TUTORIAL

The wooden mold of the tassel needs to be decorated. This is done by wrapping cords around it. You can use one cord or two if you would like to make a stripy tassel.

Materials
- Conservation glue
- Wooden tassel mold
- Embroidery scissors
- Handmade cord (see page 224)
- Strong sewing thread
- Embroidery needle

Step 1

Apply a layer of conservation glue to the mold and leave it to dry; this layer should just sink into the mold. Paint on a second layer, which will not dry as quickly as the first.

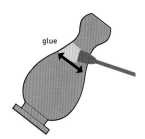

Step 2

Start to attach the cord at the foot of the mold, leaving a small tail of cord. Work around the mold, making sure that all of the cord is sitting neatly on it, and that the wraps are lying together with no gaps or glue visible. If you find that the glue is drying too quickly, apply more gradually as you work up the mold.

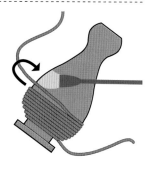

Step 3

Once you are at the top of the mold, use a dot of glue to secure the end of the cord inside the mold head. If you need to trim the cord, bind it with glue. Weave the tail of cord at the mold foot into the wraps and secure with a small dot of glue.

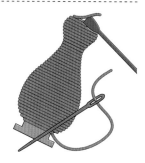

TIP

To calculate how much cord or gimp thread is needed to cover the tassel head, use string of around the same thickness as the cord you wish to use. Wrap the string around the head, from the base to the top. Mark on the string how much was needed and use that as the measure to cut your handmade cord.

RUFFS

— TUTORIAL —

Ruffs are used to cover the joins of the tassel around the top, where the head meets the suspension cord, and where the skirt meets the bottom of the head. You can make a cut or looped ruff, depending on your design. The main steps for making a ruff are the same but when making a cut ruff, use a strong sewing thread instead of the wire in Step 1.

Materials
- Knitting needle or circular object
- Wire or strong sewing thread
- Needle
- Sticky tape
- Scissors
- Boiling water (if you are making a cut ruff)

Step 1

Take a length of fine wire and a knitting needle or circular object, depending on the size of ruff required. Measure the length of ruff required using the string method (see Tip). Fold the wire in half and make a loop at the end. Tape the loop to the top of the knitting needle. Mark the length of the ruff on the needle with tape. One of the pieces of wire should lie next to the needle and the other can hang down.

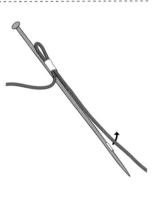

Step 2

Stick the end of the ruff to the needle. Work toward the point of the needle: wrap the threads around the needle and over one piece of wire. Do this a few times. Lift up the wire that is hanging down. Wrap it over the threads and around the wire next to the needle to form a secure loop. Ensure that both lengths of wire are taut and lying next to the needle. Continue wrapping the threads close together around the needle.

Step 3

When you reach the end mark, work one or two more wraps to ensure the ruff is long enough. Twist the two pieces of wire together to secure the wraps. Carefully remove the ruff from the knitting needle. Check that the ruff fits snugly around the join. When you are happy with the length of the ruff, secure it by weaving your thread back along its length, oversewing the wires.

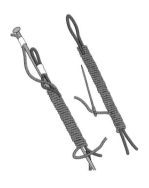

Step 4

If you are making a cut ruff, cut the loops. If it is not fluffy enough, dip it into boiling water and let it dry. Make the second ruff. The two do not both need to be the same; you could make one cut and the other looped.

SKIRT

TUTORIAL

The skirt of the tassel is formed from the threads that hang from the tassel head. These can be as long or short, or as narrow or full, as you wish. If you are using fine threads, you may need to make two skirts to balance the tassel.

Materials

- Grade C mount board/thick card
- Pencil
- Ruler
- Craft knife
- Skirt threads
- Strong sewing thread
- Embroidery needle
- Fabric and embroidery scissors
- Paper
- Sticky tape

Step 1

Make a skirt board to wrap the threads around. On the mount board, mark the length of the skirt at 1. If the thread is stretchy, add ¾ in/2 cm, and if you are going to cut it, add a little more. Add another ¾ in/2 cm to each side to hold onto while working the skirt. Measure around the head of the tassel to get the measurement of the skirt. Mark this on the board at 2. Trim off the bottom right-hand corner of the board, which will help you to remove the skirt later. Cut small slits into the board at 3 for securing the threads when not in use.

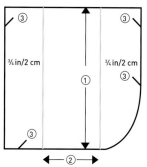

Step 2

Fold a 6½ ft/2 m length of strong sewing thread in half and create a loop over the board, making sure that the thread is lying on the left-hand pink line. Slip one of the threads under the loop and tie the two ends together. Take one thread to a slit on the left and one to a slit on the right.

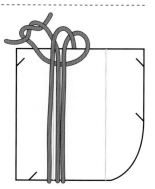

TIP

If some of the threads are twisting or not lying smoothly, boil the kettle and hold the tassel above the steam to smooth them out. Hold the skirt at eye level so that you can see the stray threads clearly.

Step 3

Slip the end of the skirt threads into the slit on the bottom of the card at 3a. Start to wrap the threads around the board. The number of times you wrap will vary depending on the thickness of the threads; the average is about four wraps. Take the spare threads down into the slit at the bottom right and tie a tight double knot around these threads. The wraps should gather up into a bunch; ensure that the first bunch is still in line with the left-hand line. The sewing thread can then be placed back into the slits at 3b and 3c. Continue to work the wraps until you get to the second pencil line. Do an extra wrap; it can be removed if the skirt is too long, but it is very difficult to add extra wraps in after.

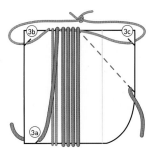

Step 4

Thread a needle with strong sewing thread and oversew along the top of the board, where the knots are, to ensure that the knots are secure and the threads cannot slip. Do not stitch the last couple of wraps; these are the ones that may not be needed once you take the skirt off the card. Gently ease the skirt off the board.

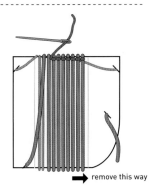

remove this way

TIP

As a general rule, the skirt should be 1–1½ times the length of the tassel head.

Step 5

If you are making a cut skirt, cut through each loop. If the ends look a little jagged, make a paper tube secured with sticky tape. Slide the tube over the tassel head and push it down so that the edge of the paper is at the ideal length for the tassels. Carefully trim the threads using sharp scissors.

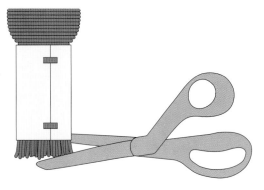

CONSTRUCTION
— TUTORIAL —

Once you have all the elements of the tassel, you can begin the construction.

Materials
- Suspension cord
- Ruffs
- Tassel head
- Tassel skirt
- Thick wire
- Pliers and wire cutters
- Wooden disk (supplied with tassel-head mold)
- Strong sewing thread
- Embroidery needle
- Embroidery scissors
- Glue

Step 1

Fold the suspension rope in half and check it is the correct length. If it is too long, trim it and bind it. Using a length of thick wire, create a coil at the end; try to make it as small and neat as possible. Sew the coil to one end of the rope, using strong sewing thread. Stitch straight through the rope to make sure it is secure.

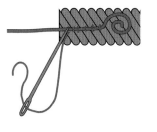

Step 2

Fold the rope in half and stitch the other end to the wire, so it is between the two pieces of rope. Insert the ends of the rope into the hole in the top of the tassel head. Put the wooden tassel-head disk around the wire and trim the wire, leaving about 1¼ in/ 3 cm. Using pliers, make a coil so that the wire cannot move.

Step 3

Attach the skirt(s) using the ends of the sewing thread left from making the skirt. Wrap the skirt around the tassel-head base and ensure that it is as tight as possible, using the looped thread. Tie a knot to keep the skirt in place, and put a small dab of glue on to the knot. Trim off the ends of the threads. Repeat this step for the second skirt.

Step 4

Attach the ruffs in the same way, ensuring that they join and are pulled tight. If you are using a wire for the ruff, twist to secure it. Leave a tail of ½ in/13 mm. Push the tail toward the tassel head and bury it.

DECORATIONS
TUTORIAL

Decorations such as feathers, beads, embroidered shapes, pompoms, or mini tassels can be added to the tassel.

Materials
- Tape measure/ruler
- Thread/cord
- Thin wire
- Embroidery scissors
- Embellishments
- Glue

Step 1

Measure around the join of the tassel skirt and make a note of that measurement. Plan out the order of decorations, leaving consistent gaps between each one.

Step 2

Attach the decorations to a thread or cord then attach these to a piece of thin wire. Twist the wire around the threads to secure them.

Step 3

Wrap the wire with the decorations around the skirt of the tassel before the ruff is attached. Secure the wire by twisting it and applying a small amount of glue to hold it in place.

TIP
Once your tassel is finished, hang it up for a while to allow the threads to settle.

HAND QUILTING

In quilting, two layers of fabric, usually with an insulating layer between them, are sewn together with multiple rows of stitches. Quilting designs vary widely and may be figural or geometric. Quilts are generally made as bedcovers or wall hangings. With the huge range of printed calicos available, quilting has become a popular and versatile technique.

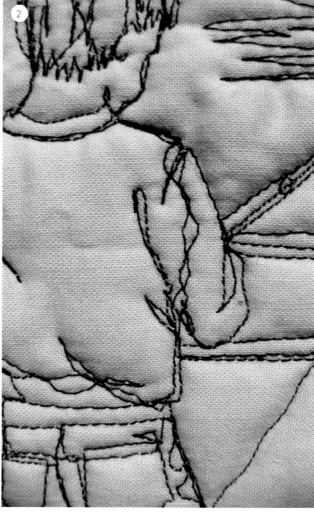

Quilting can be traced back to medieval Europe (5th to 15th centuries); there is evidence of quilts being used as protective wear under armor. It was often in the form of leather padded with sheep's wool or straw.

By the 17th century hand quilting had become popular, and skilled needle workers created a variety of quilted items, such as bedcovers and clothing, and silk doublets and breeches for wealthy courtiers. Later, ladies' petticoats, men's waistcoats, jackets, and babies' caps were also quilted. Quilting became popular in colonial America, from the 17th century.

Until the mid-19th century, quilts were very time consuming to produce and expensive to buy, which made these textiles strictly luxury items. Quilting during this time was not a common hobby; it was mostly wealthy women who had time to spend on quilting. Much time was spent spinning and weaving to create fabric for quilting.

The Industrial Revolution of the 18th and 19th centuries made fabrics more widely accessible and affordable, and quilting saw an increase in popularity, especially in the USA. Women produced beautiful quilts by combining new printed cottons—some of which were made especially for quilting—with old fabrics already in their possession. The 19th century was the golden age of American quilting.

The 1970s saw a quilting revival, and in the 1980s, timesaving techniques, particularly the rotary cutter and strip piecing, sped up the process. Quilting is popular in North America, Europe, Australia, New Zealand, and Japan. A wide variety of printed cottons and designs are available for quilting, with some quilters focusing on traditional work and others developing innovative techniques.

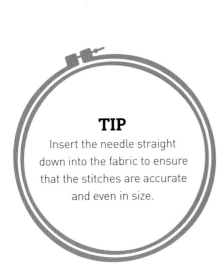

TIP
Insert the needle straight down into the fabric to ensure that the stitches are accurate and even in size.

3

Three-Dimensional Embroidery

QUILTING PRIMER

TYPES OF QUILTING

English quilting For this, your chosen fabric lies on top of a filling fabric, also called wadding, which creates a raised texture, with a fine backing fabric at the bottom.

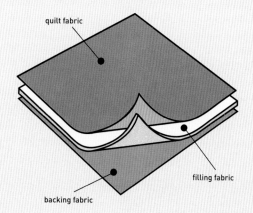

quilt fabric

filling fabric

backing fabric

Trapunto This also uses two fabrics: a quilt fabric and a fine cotton backing, with wadding inserted into a stitched shape or pattern. The backing is added to hide areas that have been stuffed.

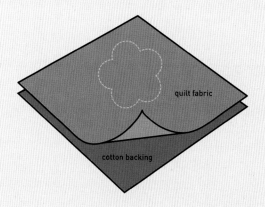

quilt fabric

cotton backing

Italian quilting This uses two fabrics: your quilt fabric and a fine cotton backing, with wadding inserted along tunnels created with running stitch.

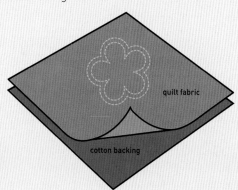

quilt fabric

cotton backing

Crazy patchwork This creative form of quilting has no strict rules. You can use any scraps of fabric, threads, buttons, or embellishments. Decorative stitching is worked along the line where the fabrics meet and a fine-cotton backing fabric is attached by hand or machine.

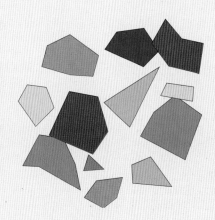

FABRICS

Cotton is the most common fabric used for quilts, since it is available in a huge range of colors and prints. Cotton is easy to work with because it is soft to sew through. Silk or linen also work well, but often the thick fabric makes the quilting less obvious. If you are unsure of how a fabric will look, try working a small sample before you start the main piece. If you are going to make a piece of clothing, check that the fabric is washable.

SHAPES

If you want to work shapes on to the fabric, it is best to draw them out first. Depending on the design and fabric used, you can either draw them on the back or the front of the fabric.

THREADS

For English quilting, the thread goes through three layers of fabric, so it is best to use a strong thread that matches the color of the fabric. Start threads with a small knot on the back of the fabric to keep the front neat.

STITCHES

Make sure the stitches are evenly spaced and of a consistent size, and that they go vertically through the layers. Working quilting in a frame is a good idea because it helps to keep the stitches straight.

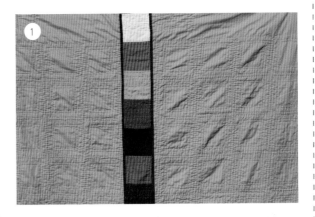

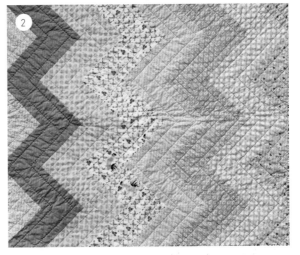

ITALIAN QUILTING
— TUTORIAL —

You can use Italian quilting on its own or combine it with English quilting, working the background in rows of Italian quilting and the shapes in the foreground in English quilting. If you want to follow an existing pattern on a fabric, detailed patterns are best avoided: it is hard to work rows of running stitch alongside complex patterns and you will lose the delicate feel once you have pulled the wool through the tunnels.

Materials
- Fine cotton backing
- Pencil
- Plain or patterned fabric (any)
- Matching sewing thread
- Embroidery needle
- Embroidery scissors
- Quilting wool
- Blunt tapestry needle that fits quilting wool

Step 1

See page 234 for positioning the two fabrics. Draw an outline of your shape on the backing fabric, and then a second outline around this. Ensure that the gap between the lines is consistent in width as these mark the channel you will fill. With printed fabrics, you can simply follow the printed patterns.

Step 2

Place your top fabric onto your backing fabric and, using an embroidery needle, work a running stitch onto both of the drawn lines.

Step 3

Using a long length of the quilting wool in a blunt tapestry needle, pass from the back of the piece, through the channel and around the whole shape.

TIP
To prevent the work from puckering or shrinking when washed, bring the wool to the surface of the back of the piece frequently and leave a tiny loop of wool to allow for movement. This is particularly important on shapes that are angled or detailed.

TRAPUNTO

— TUTORIAL —

Trapunto is often worked along with English quilting (see page 238). You can work the background with English quilting and the foreground with trapunto. You can work the patterns on a fabric in the same way but you do not need to draw on the design. It is best to work on large designs or select particular ones to use. This will produce a bold design that is easy to stuff.

Materials
- Plain or patterned fabric (any)
- Fine cotton backing
- Pins
- Pencil
- Matching sewing thread
- Embroidery needle
- Embroidery scissors
- Fine cotton backing
- Wadding or wool
- Mellor

Step 1

Draw the shape on to the fine cotton backing. Place the top fabric over the fine cotton and pin them together.

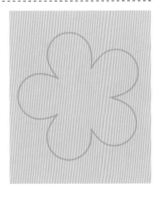

Step 2

Work a running stitch through the fabric and the fine cotton along the outline you have drawn.

Step 3

Cut a small slit in the fine cotton backing within the design shape. Stuff the wadding into the shape, making sure that it reaches all of the corners. You can use a mellor to gently guide the wadding into awkward-to-reach areas.

Step 4

Sew up the slit.

ENGLISH QUILTING
—○— TUTORIAL —○—

English quilting is a simple form of quilting, created by working a running or backstitch in a repeat pattern. A range of different patterns can be worked, or if you are using a printed fabric, you can use the shapes on it to produce raised areas (see Italian quilting on page 236). You will need your chosen fabric, wadding, and a backing fabric behind that. The thickness of the quilting will be determined by the thickness of the wadding.

Materials
- Pencil
- Template for the pattern
- Fine cotton backing
- Fabric (any)
- Wadding
- Thread to match fabric
- Embroidery needle
- Embroidery and paper scissors

Shell pattern

You need a template to create a shell pattern. Place it on your top fabric and draw around it. Layer your backing, wadding, and top fabrics, then work a running stitch around the lines.

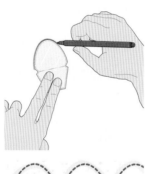

Diamond pattern

Create the diamonds by working straight lines in one direction and then in the opposite direction.

TIP
You can combine these patterns to create your own designs. Make sure the stitches are small and pulled tight so that you achieve the raised areas.

Wine-glass pattern

Use a circle template to
create geometric patterns,
tracing around it in the
same way as for the
shell pattern.

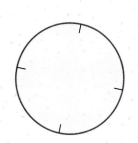

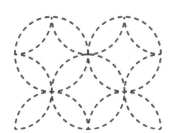

Fabric patterns

Use the pattern on the fabric,
either all of the shapes and
lines or just selected lines.
Work a running stitch
along them.

Selected shapes

Cut out templates and place
them on the fabric. Draw
around them on to the
fabric and work stitches
over the top.

CRAZY PATCHWORK
— TUTORIAL —

You can use crazy patchwork to make cushions, bags, or pieces of artwork. If you are making up an item with the patchwork, remember to incorporate a seam allowance. This tutorial is for hand application but if you want to use a machine, sew the pieces of fabric together on the reverse, and then turn the fabric over.

Materials
- Pre-washed firm-weave fabric, such as fine cotton
- Assorted small pieces of textured fabric, such as cottons, silks, organza, velvet, and linen
- Old doilies and hankies, embroidered or printed
- Small pieces of embroidery or cross stitch or stitching samples
- Silk and satin ribbons, lace, and braids
- Embroidery threads, such as stranded cottons, metallic threads, silks, or wools
- Beads, sequins, and buttons
- Strong sewing thread
- Embroidery scissors
- Embroidery needles

Step 1

Gather all of the pieces of fabric you would like to use; they do not need to match and should be of all different shapes and sizes. Cut the backing fabric to size, allowing extra if you are planning to mount the patchwork as artwork.

Step 2

The first piece of fabric can be any size, although it is helpful if it has more than four sides. Place the fabric on to the backing and pin in place. Do not put it in the middle because this will encourage you to think about symmetry, which is not required. Place it the right way up.

Step 3

The second piece of fabric should have an edge the same length as one edge of the first piece. Place it upside down on top of the first piece of fabric. Work a running stitch through both pieces of fabric and the backing fabric, about ¼ in/ 6 mm from the edges. Flip the second piece of fabric over, so that the correct side is visible.

Step 4

Continue to work around the applied pieces in this way, each time putting the next piece of fabric on to the already applied areas upside down. Work until the entire backing fabric is covered.

Step 5

Work decorative stitches along the joins of two fabrics, such as feather or chain stitch (see page 28), or French knots (see page 33). You can also add buttons or beads.

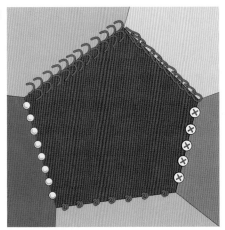

TIP
If you have any gaps or puckers in your patchwork, do not panic—you can cover them with a piece of lace, a button, or an outline stitch.

EVA FULINOVA
PROFILE

Eva makes textile jewelry. She is inspired by the intricate needlework seen on historic textiles, glimpses of nature in the city, romance, and fairytale elements in everyday life.

A typical piece starts life as a long strip of white silk, which Eva dyes a base color with natural dyes. Then she pleats and overdyes it repeatedly to create an effect that resembles the complex colors seen in nature—a green leaf with a browned edge or the blues of a black crow's feather. She pleats the fabric by hand (by sewing rows of running stitch) and uses smocking to hold the pleats together and create textures. When smocking, she often adds

----

"I'm inspired by the colors of nature as they change through the seasons."

----

small glass beads to look like seeds or drops of water. The piece is then completed with silver wire and chain, depending on the design.

Eva works with fine silk, which lends itself well to the small scale of the work and the delicate pleating. It's also a material that takes natural dyes beautifully and easily. She uses stranded cotton threads for smocking. Eva is always looking for unusual colors, sometimes using vintage skeins or dyeing them herself.

Dyeing is the longest part of the process, sometimes taking days or even weeks, depending on the dye used. Eva likes to dye blue in her indigo vat, doing it the old, slow way by fermentation, which takes patience, experience, and often luck. Pleating and smocking a piece typically takes her several hours. Her most challenging smocking task was making a necklace that had the text of a poem in between its tiny pleats. The aim was to make the lines legible, so it needed to be folded and smocked very precisely.

"I like to make most things from scratch, including the clasps on necklaces and hooks for earrings."

Eva exhibits her smocking work online. She keeps a blog about dyeing, growing dye plants, her process, and inspirations. Thanks to the Internet, she can show her work to a worldwide audience. Eva sells through an online shop that she runs herself. Because she mostly makes one-of-a-kind pieces in very limited numbers, this suits her perfectly—and fortunately, she enjoys photographing her work.

Specialty
Smocked jewelry

Inspired by
Vintage textiles and romantic and fairytale moments

Experiments with
Dyeing fabric, which she then smocks

Most challenging project
Smocked necklace that contained text from a poem

Top tip
Dye your own fabrics to create particularly unique pieces.

Shop
Jewelry made to order (http://tinctory.co.uk)

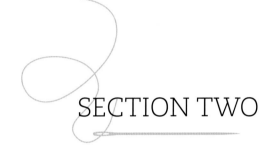

SECTION TWO

MACHINE EMBROIDERY

Digital machine embroidery worked on artists' canvas
by Michelle Matthews.

CHAPTER 7

FREE-MOTION EMBROIDERY

Free-motion machine embroidery is any embroidery
done using a sewing machine that is not computerized.
The stitches are created by the user of the sewing
machine, so these techniques require skill and
precision. Most sewing machines are able to create
free-motion embroidery but you will need practice
to ensure that you know how to set up the machine
correctly. It is also important to place the fabric in
a ring to protect your fingers from the needle.

1. Free-motion machine embroidery, hand surface stitching, and needle felting using silk, cotton, rayon, and wool threads on wool *by Michala Gyetvai.*
2. Free-motion machine embroidery over a digital print using cotton and polyester threads on cotton drill *by Gillian Bates.*
3. Free-motion machine embroidery, hand surface stitching, and needle felting using silk, cotton, rayon, and wool threads on wool *by Michala Gyetvai.*

1. Free-motion machine embroidery and needle felting using silk, cotton, rayon, and wool on a wool background *by Michala Gyetvai*.
2. Free-motion machine-embroidered landscape worked on cotton canvas fabric with cotton and rayon threads *by Monika Kinner-Whalen*.
3. Free-motion machine-embroidered landscape worked on cotton canvas with beading *by Monika Kinner-Whalen*.
4. Free-motion machine embroidery using Guttermann threads on linen *by Josie Rossington*.
5. Free-motion machine embroidery and appliqué shapes *by Joanne Melrose*.
6. Free-motion machine embroidery using polyester and metallic threads on velvet and silk *by Leisa Rich*.

1. Free-motion machine embroidery using polyester and metallic threads on mixed media *by Leisa Rich.*
2. Detail of figure 1.
3. Free-motion machine embroidery on appliquéd printed cotton *by Joanne Melrose.*

3

OVERVIEW

Free-motion machine embroidery is created
on a sewing machine but the user controls the
machine carefully and therefore the result. The fabric,
secured in a hoop, is skilfully moved under the
needle to create a design to embellish clothing,
household items, and textile art. As with hand
embroidery, the possibilities are endless.

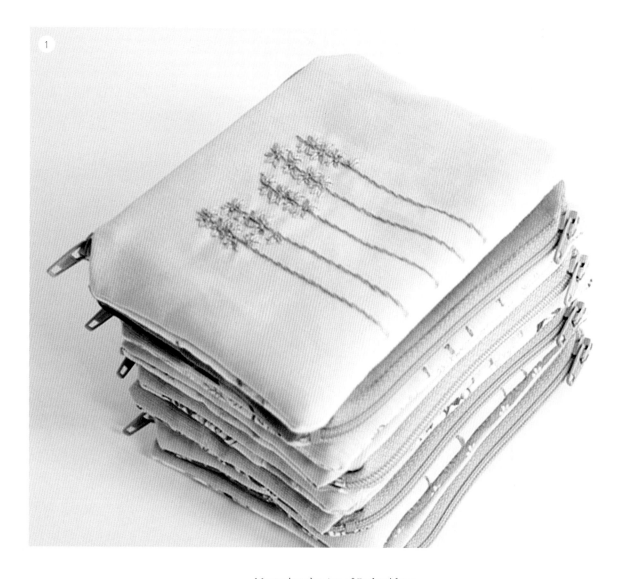

1

1. Free-motion machine embroidery using cotton floss on cotton and cotton canvas *by Eva Vercauteren.*
2. Free-motion machine embroidery of a hummingbird with hand-cut areas worked onto jersey fabric *by Lana Rabinovich.*
3. Handmade purse with appliqué and free-motion machine embroidery worked on linen *by Viv Sliwka.*

Throughout history, embroidered embellishments were considered to be an indication of wealth; this was because embroideries were hand stitched and extremely time consuming. Each design, although following a certain theme or trend, was unique and therefore highly valuable to the embroiderer and the wearer.

The first embroidery machine was invented by Josué Heilmann in 1828. The machine made it possible to replicate hand-worked embroidery at a much faster rate and work that would have taken weeks or even months to complete by hand could be done in a fraction of the time by machine. Yet Heilmann sold only two of these machines because, quite understandably, embroiderers felt threatened by this invention. In 1863 Isaac Groebli invented a different type of embroidery machine that led to the development of the automatic Schiffli machine, which could stitch in all directions. The invention of the eye-pointed sewing-machine needle by Walter Hunt in 1934 was the start of modern-day home-machine embroidery.

Although a sewing machine is used, free-motion embroidery is also a manual process. Each design is unique and cannot be reproduced accurately. Even for the very talented sewing artist, the creation of complex designs and patterns is time consuming, especially because the machine has to be rethreaded manually each time the color is changed. Yet for craft enthusiasts today, creating unique embroidered pieces on a free-motion machine is important. Although computerized embroidery enables accuracy and duplication, many people believe in the individuality of a manually worked piece—for the beauty of the work and its value to the buyer.

The vast choice of fabrics and threads offers many possibilities for free-motion embroidery. For example, a range of new fibers, such as dissolvable fabric, allow you to make lacelike fabrics by stitching free motion and then soaking the piece in water, which leaves only the threads. With free-motion embroidery, you can create elaborate monograms or shapes, or entire landscapes.

2

3

Free-Motion Embroidery

CABLE STITCH
—◦— TUTORIAL —◦—

Cable stitch offers the chance to experiment with threads not normally used for machine embroidery. You use a smooth hand-embroidery thread, such as stranded cotton, perle, knitting wool, or silk, in the bobbin, and work the stitch on the back of the fabric. Use cable stitch alone or to create details on top of other stitching.

Materials
- Fabric (any)
- Erasable marker
- Sewing machine
- Ring frame
- Polyester or cotton thread
- Selection of smooth hand-embroidery threads
- Embroidery scissors

Step 1

Draw a design on the wrong side of the fabric and place it, design-side up, in the ring frame. Use polyester 50 or cotton for the top thread and a hand-embroidery thread for the bobbin thread. Wind the bobbin by hand and place it in the bobbin case. Practice, then try the following effects.

Long-stitch effect

Move the hoop very quickly while stitching so the stitches are very long. This is a way of creating a quick background. A number of different threads can be worked separately to create a highly textured area.

Hand-couched effect

Move the hoop at a medium speed so that the perle thread looks as if it has been hand couched (see page 37). Machine-stitched couching is much faster than hand couching and allows you to create a detailed picture relatively quickly.

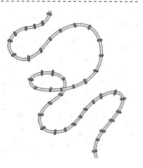

Wide-couched effect

Move the hoop very slowly so that the top thread covers more of the perle. In this example, carefully consider the color of your cotton or polyester top thread because it will be far more prominent when sewn at a slow speed.

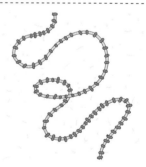

VERMICELLI

— TUTORIAL —

Vermicelli stitch is a machine line that meanders around in curves, going inward and outward. You can work it in single rows or pairs of rows. It can also be used to cover an area, forming a background for further embroidery work on top.

Materials

- Fabric (any)
- Ring frame
- Sewing machine
- Thread
- Embroidery scissors

Step 1

Place the fabric in a ring frame. Set the stitch length and width to 0. Hold the top and bobbin threads taut.

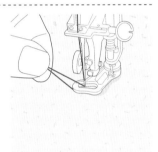

Step 2

Stitch a small leaflike shape. Move the frame to stitch another immediately beside it.

Step 3

Continue to move the frame, creating more leaflike shapes. Move the frame rhythmically and at an even speed to fill the fabric with vermicelli stitch and create a patterned surface.

TIP

Always work a sample. Threads all have different tensions and you will need to adjust both the top and bottom to achieve the desired effect.

TIP

Try using different colors of thread to add more interest; a variegated thread works extremely well because the subtle changes in color show up in the stitches.

DISSOLVABLE FABRIC
— TUTORIAL —

Dissolvable fabric can be used so that the embroidery you create with your sewing machine does not have fabric behind it. The dissolvable fabric is worked in the ring frame, and the machine stitching creates the image or pattern. The "fabric" you create with stitches can be used to build up a surface or to create a motif. This tutorial shows you how to make a simple bowl.

Materials
- Sewing machine
- Dissolvable fabric
- Erasable marker
- Ring frame
- Threads
- Embroidery scissors
- Polystyrene board—optional
- Cold water
- PVA glue

Step 1

Set up the machine as instructed. Put two layers of cold-water dissolvable fabric in the ring frame. This fabric tears easily so start with two layers until you are confident; then you can use one layer.

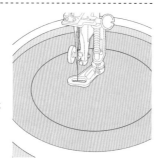

Step 2

Remember that both sides will be visible, so plan the colors you will use before you start. Draw a circle on your fabric as a guide. Machine-sew straight lines radiating out from the center to give the piece structure and strength. Draw some guidelines onto the dissolvable fabric to help you when stitching.

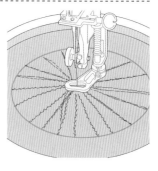

Step 3

Start spiraling out from the middle of the circle. Do not make the stitches too long and try to overlap a few rows to ensure that the entire bowl is connected.

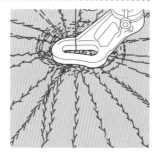

Step 4

Fill in the whole circle, changing color as you get nearer the edge to achieve a striped effect. You can work a number of layers of stitches to make a denser embroidery.

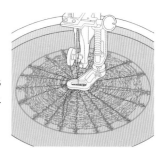

Step 5

Take the embroidery out of the frame. Cut it out close to the stitching and trim any loose threads.

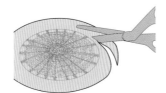

Step 6

Rinse the embroidery in cold water. Leave some of the stickiness in the embroidery, which will help it to keep its shape when dry. This is especially important if you are creating a 3D piece.

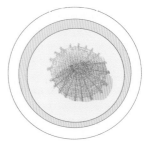

Step 7

Leave the embroidery to dry over a mold to form a bowl shape (the embroidery will take the shape of any 3D object) or dry it flat if you want to make a flat piece of lacelike fabric.

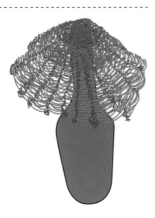

Step 8

The bowl is ready when it is completely dry. You can paint it with PVA glue to protect and strengthen it.

TIP

If you tear your fabric as you stitch you can easily add another patch. Remember that the bobbin thread will be visible on your final piece.

TIP

If the embroidery is very delicate, pin it to a polystyrene board so that it keeps its shape as the dissolvable fabric vanishes.

TIP

If you wish to produce a flat piece of lacelike fabric, work the machine in repeat patterns, making sure that the stitches are all linked.

WHIPSTITCH

━━● TUTORIAL ●━━

Whipstitch creates a textured surface. The bobbin thread is brought up to cover the top thread, so that the top thread is not as visible: it "whips" around the top thread. This stitch can be used to create shapes and images, working in straight lines or curves. You can also use it to create textured backgrounds that could have additional stitching on top.

Materials
- Sewing machine
- Sewing thread
- Fabric (any)
- Ring frame
- Rayon or metallic thread in a contrasting color
- Embroidery scissors

Step 1

Set up the machine with a sewing thread as the top thread and the top tension tight. Set the bobbin thread at medium tension. Set the machine to zigzag stitch of ¹⁄₁₆ in/1.5 mm length and ¹⁄₈ in/3 mm width. Place the fabric in the ring frame.

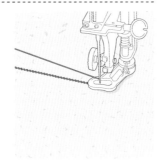

Step 2

It is essential to move the frame very slowly. The bobbin thread will come to the top and "whip" itself around the top thread. Make sure that you do not stay in one spot too long because the top thread may snap.

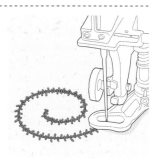

Step 3

Move the frame in a circular direction to create a spiral, working round and round in one continuous line.

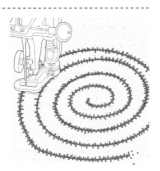

Step 4

Alternatively, work the whipstitch in lines that are very close together.

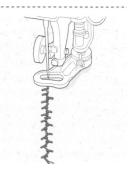

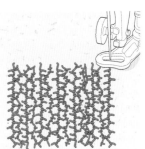

STRAIGHT FILLING STITCH

TUTORIAL

Straight filling stitch is a good exercise to practice to get to know your machine. It is a series of straight stitches worked in rows to fill a shape or design. Try to keep the stitches a consistent size; this is easier to achieve when working smaller stitches because there is less thread being pulled through the needle. With practice, you can move on to longer stitches and work more quickly.

Materials
- Sewing machine
- Erasable marker
- Fabric (any)
- Ring frame
- Sewing thread in different colors
- Embroidery scissors

Step 1

Set up the machine as instructed. Set the stitch length and width to 0, straight stitch setting. Draw the shape you will fill in on the surface of your fabric. Place the fabric in the ring frame.

Step 2

Start stitching and move the frame to create lines. Work up to the lines you have drawn.

Step 3

Choose the effect that you prefer for your design. If you move the hoop slowly and have a fast machine speed, you will create a small, tight stitch. Moving the hoop fast will result in a long, loose stitch.

Step 4

Continue to fill in the shape to the density you require. Make sure the surface is even and you do not have a buildup of threads in one particular place.

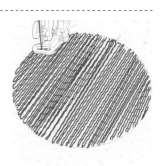

Step 5

Use another color to create the effect of shading. If you have a neutral or medium-tone color in your bobbin spool you do not have to change the color of the bobbin.

CAROL SHINN
— PROFILE —

Carol is inspired by the variety she sees in the physical world around her. Her current work focuses on the natural landscape as well as on the aging and decay of buildings and other human artifacts. She concentrates on tactile surfaces and the visual changes brought on by time, and the moods evoked by place.

Carol makes all her pieces in machine embroidery, using a home sewing machine. Her process begins with

---

"I try to make each piece a new challenge. Sometimes this means a change in the direction of stitching or a particular color gradation that I know will be difficult."

---

photographs, which she takes herself. She alters them on the computer and transfers them to fabric. Then she stitches the piece with a basic sewing machine. None of the stitching process is computerized. The stitches, which completely cover her canvas, are like pencil hatching. Carol lowers the feed dog so she can move the fabric freely to achieve the length and density of the stitch she wants. She layers different colors of thread throughout each piece to enrich the colors. The stitching is so dense that none of the original image or fabric shows. The time she spends on each piece can range from one week to two months.

In terms of materials, Carol sews on a base of 10 oz/283 g cotton duck (canvas) with sizing. This is sold as canvas for painters. She uses many brands of cotton and polyester thread, mostly around 1½ oz/45 g in weight, but no shiny or metallic threads.

Carol exhibits her work with two galleries in the USA: the Hibberd McGrath Gallery in Breckenridge, CO, and the Jane Sauer Gallery in Santa Fe, NM. The Jane Sauer

> "Allow yourself to be obsessive and passionate about this one part of your life. There are no shortcuts."

Gallery takes her work to various expos in the country sponsored by SOFA/The Art Fair Company, Inc. She also exhibits at various invitational shows.

Carol advises that being alone is the only way you can become "one with your work." Allow yourself to observe the smallest of details and the complexity of each color, thinking about mixing several colors of thread rather than just putting down one color.

Specialty
Machine embroidery

Inspired by
The world around her

Experiments with
Creating machine-hatching on canvas to create detailed shading

Most challenging project
Every project has its own challenges

Top tip
Make sure you have the time and space to work undisturbed.

Shop
Galleries and made to order
(http://www.carolshinn.com)

CHAPTER 8

DIGITAL EMBROIDERY

Digital machine embroidery refers to embroidery
that is worked on a computerized machine. You upload
a design with the information that the machine
requires to stitch the design. Little user input is
needed, although you may need to change the color
of the thread if the design requires more than one
color. Software is also available that allows you to
create your own design files so that the work is unique.
This enables you to create mass embroideries using
one design, which offers commercial possibilities.

1. Digital machine embroidery using cotton threads on linen *by Lana Rabinovich.*
2. Digital machine embroidery using rayon threads on linen *by Lana Rabinovich.*
3. Digital machine embroidery using cotton threads on cotton *by Amersham Fabrics* (design and photo by David Lum).

1

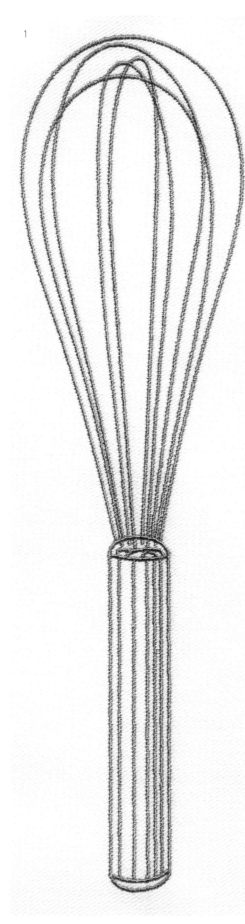

2

3

1. Digital machine embroidery using cotton threads on cotton *by Amersham Fabrics* (design and photo by David Lum).
2. Digital machine embroidery using cotton threads on linen *by Lana Rabinovich*.
3. Machine-embroidered personalized napkins *by Peter and Penny Ellis*.
4. Digital machine embroidery using Isacord threads on canvas *by Michelle Matthews*.

1. Digital machine embroidery using Isacord threads on canvas *by Michelle Matthews.*
2. Digital machine embroidery using polycotton threads on linen *by Heather Shaw.*
3. Digital machine embroidery using Isacord threads on canvas *by Michelle Matthews.*
4. Digital machine embroidery using polycotton threads on linen *by Heather Shaw* (photo by Erin Riley).

③

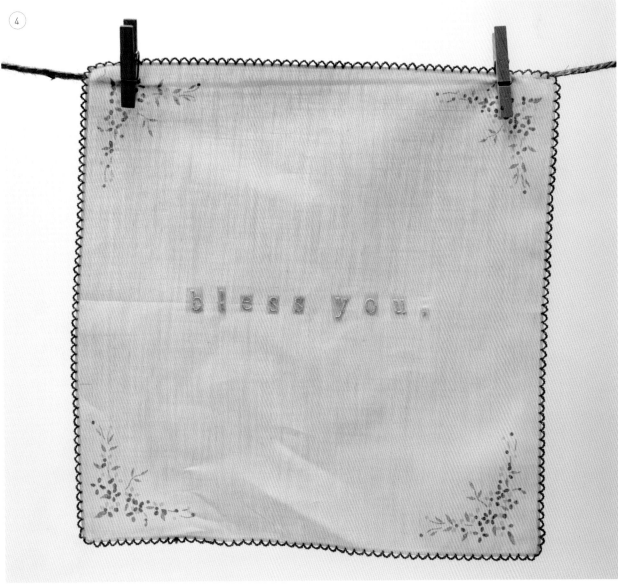

④

OVERVIEW

Digital software has enabled embroidery enthusiasts to create the finest of embroidery patterns; the work is done automatically. The user simply needs to change the color of the threads as required. Clothing, bags, hats, wall art, and household items can be easily embellished with beautiful embroideries.

1. Digital machine-embroidered stylized rose in cotton thread *by Urban Threads*.
2. Digital machine-embroidered luggage tag in cotton thread *by Urban Threads*.

Before computers were commonplace and affordable, most machine embroideries were produced by a process called "punching." The design was constructed on paper, which was run through a mechanical machine that punched the design through the paper and into the fabric with thread. This was very time-consuming, and the slightest error could ruin the design; the whole piece would have to be started again. Modern-day embroidery digitizing is called "punching" in reference to this original process.

The first computer-graphics embroidery design system was created in 1980, and was run on a minicomputer. The designer could create the pattern in the computer, print it off onto paper, and run it through the embroidery machine.

In the late 1980s, major embroidery-machine companies adapted the commercial systems and marketed them for home use. Since the late 1990s, as computers have become more affordable, computerized home-machine embroidery has grown in popularity, along with computerized embroidery-digitizing programs and machines. Home embroidery enthusiasts have access to a selection of disks with various patterns from independent pattern and machine manufacturers as well as free downloads from many embroidery sites on the Internet, providing a huge choice of embellishment options.

TIP
Start by buying designs online. Once you gain confidence, you can try creating your own designs.

DIGITAL EMBROIDERY PRIMER

For digital machine embroidery, you need a computerized sewing machine. Most modern sewing machines are computer controlled. The framed area of fabric is held under the sewing needle, which moves automatically to create the design. The amount of user input required depends on your machine. Non-industrial machines generally have one needle and therefore you will need to change the thread while working the embroidery if you want a different color. The number of times you have to do this depends on the complexity of your design.

BUYING DESIGNS

When you buy a design, make sure the file is in the correct format for your machine. The file contains all of the information needed to create the design—stitch data and machine functions.

Appliqué is possible with digital machine embroidery. When buying a design, note whether it requires a piece of fabric to be applied to it. The design has all the steps programmed in, so it will stop when the fabric has been applied and requires trimming by the user.

STITCHES

You can work many different stitches, depending on the capability of your machine. It is worth experimenting with different types of stitches before you start a project. It is important to get to know your machine so that you can use it to its full potential. Making small samples is a great way to experiment and learn.

STABILIZERS

A stabilizer is used to support and stabilize fabric while you are sewing and helps to keep it taut, preventing puckers or wrinkles. There are several types of stabilizers. The type you choose depends on the fabric, the nature of the design, and the purpose of the finished piece. If you are unsure which to use, try out the options on a sample first. The main types are listed below.

Tear-away is ideal for medium-weight fabrics such as cotton. If you are creating a large, complex design, use two layers of stabilizer. Once the design is complete, you can tear away the stabilizer. Ensure you do this slowly to avoid damaging the embroidery by pulling out stitches from the design.

Cutaway is ideal for stretchy fabrics such as knits and fleece. Use two layers for a large design. Once the design is complete, you can cut away the excess stabilizer.

Iron-on is ideal for most lightweight fabrics. Once the embroidery is complete, tear or peel off the excess. Be aware that the glue can leave some stickiness on the machine needle, so clean it before working on another piece.

DIGITAL EMBROIDERY
TUTORIAL

In digital machine embroidery, a design is programmed into a computerized sewing machine, and the computer sends commands to the needle. The designs can be your own, or you can purchase them online.

Materials

- Digital embroidery design file
- Computerized sewing machine with hoop
- Sewing threads
- Fabric (any)
- Stabilizer or interfacing
- Embroidery scissors

Step 1

Choose the design file. Select the correct threads and colors for the design. Load the design on to your machine. Put a stabilizer or interfacing behind the fabric (see facing page). Secure the fabric in the hoop.

Step 2

Begin your embroidery.

Step 3

Home machines require you to monitor the embroidery. You will have to change the thread color manually. There are often gaps between areas filled with the same color. For these you need to take the thread over the gap to the new area, and cut the thread where it "jumps" when you have finished with that color.

TIP

Once the machine has finished, you can remove the embroidery and neaten up the jumps by finishing them off by hand.

URBAN THREADS
PROFILE

Urban Threads primarily make machine embroidery; they create the digital image files that instruct an embroidery machine how to recreate their original artworks in stitches. Although the market is dominated by traditional and safe designs—teddy bears and flowers—Urban Threads think the medium can be used in far more creative ways. They experiment with new techniques and styles, such as layering sheer, open-fill stitches to replicate watercolor washes, and creating light meandering running stitches meant to resemble freehand machine embroidery.

> "Machine embroidery is not the same as hand embroidery. There are things it can do that hand embroidery cannot, and the reverse is true too."

Urban Threads are inspired by contemporary and modern art. They love to do something fresh and unexpected with every design, whether it's experimental digitizing techniques, or exploring themes such as tattoos, steampunk, and Gothic designs that are traditionally ignored by the industry. They also look to classic hand-embroidery techniques and aesthetics, to see how they can render them in modern styles.

The team gathers together every fortnight to discuss new themes and design ideas. Designers traditionally start with a hand-drawn sketch, which may go through a series of revisions to make sure the design is both artistically sound and will translate well into stitches. Once the pencil sketch is approved, it is scanned into the computer.

The artist redraws the image in a vector program, adding details and color, as well as technical cues for the digitizer. The finished image is printed for the digitizer, who renders it in a professional digitizing program, taking into account density, stitch count, trims, and underlays. It is a partnership between these two artists to create the final piece.

1. Digital machine-embroidered book cover worked onto a linen background.
2. Digital machine embroidered onto cotton fabric.
3. Digital machine-embroidered twill made into a cushion.

"I love creating embroidery designs that are designed with a purpose, to have shapes and forms and texture that are meant to be used and worn in certain ways." Niamh O'Connor, Art Director

When the design is done, a sample is stitched out on an embroidery machine to see how the work translates from the computer.

From concept to completion, a single design takes two to three days. Drawing a large, complex design can often take an artist two to three hours with revisions, and digitizing that design can take about four hours. Stitching out the art usually takes another hour.

Specialty
Digital machine-embroidered pieces

Inspired by
Modern and contemporary art

Experiments with
Creating modern designs using a range of techniques

Most challenging aspect
What works on screen does not always work on the textile.

Top tip
When designing your piece, remember that the embroidery will be raised from the fabric.

Shop
www.urbanthreads.com

RESOURCES

Hand embroidery using cotton and floss on polished cotton *by Sarah Homfray*.

SUPPLIERS

The Beadshop
www.the-beadshop.co.uk
Beads

DMC Creative World
www.dmc.com
Threads and fabric

eQuilter
www.equilter.com
Fabric and threads

Fireside Stitchery
www.firesidestitchery.com
Threads, canvas, equipment, and gold threads

Hedgehog Handworks
www.hedgehoghandworks.com
Threads and equipment

John James
www.jjneedles.com
Needles

MacCulloch and Wallis
www.macculloch-wallis.co.uk
Trimmings, threads, and fabric

Needle in a Haystack
www.needlestack.com
Frames, threads, equipment, ribbon, beads, and buttons

Nordic Needle
www.nordicneedle.com
Frames, fabric, and threads

Pearsalls Embroidery Silks
www.pearsallsembroidery.co.uk
Silk threads

Rittenhouse Needlepoint
www.rittenhouseneedlepoint.com
Threads and equipment

The Silk Route
www.thesilkroute.co.uk
Silk fabric

Sophie Long
www.sophielong.co.uk
Kits, supplies, and embroidery frames and trestles

Stitching Bits and Bobs
www.stitchingbitsandbobs.com

Stitchin' Post
www.stitchinpost.com
Fabric

Thistle threads
www.thistle-threads.com
Threads

Toye Kenning and Spencer/Benton and Johnson
www.toye.com
Metal threads

Willow Fabrics
www.willowfabrics.com
All embroidery supplies—threads and fabric

www.coatscrafts.com
Threads and fabric

www.embroiderysupplies.com
Frames and needles

www.josyrose.com
Jewels, beads, ribbons, and sequins

www.knitandsew.co.uk
Haberdashery and sewing shop

www.spoiltrottenbeads.co.uk
Beads

1. Hand embroidery using cotton floss on linen
by Jazmin Berakha.

USEFUL WEBSITES

www.sophielong.co.uk
Author's website, with details about her work

www.ddaymuseum.co.uk/overlord.htm
Overlord embroidery, commemorating D-Day,
in Portsmouth, UK

www.egausa.org
Information on local guilds in the USA

www.embroiderersguild.com
Information about local guilds in the UK

www.embroiderersguild.com/magazines/index.php
Embroidery magazines produced by the Embroiderers'
Guild

www.etsy.com
Market for handmade and vintage goods

www.handembroidery.ning.com
A network for hand embroidery artists

www.interweave.com/needle/piecework_magazine
Covers a wide variety of needlework, with each issue
focusing on a particular theme

www.metmuseum.org
The Metropolitan Museum of Art, New York, which
includes embroidery collections

www.quiltersclubofamerica.com
Quilters' club of America, USA

www.quiltingdaily.com/blogs/quiltingarts
Quilting Arts Magazine, available in print and digital forms

www.royal-needlework.org.uk
Information about this international center for teaching,
practicing, and promoting hand embroidery across a wide
range of techniques

www.selvedge.org
Magazine, shop, and online community for textiles in
fashion, fine art, and interiors

www.smocking.org
Smocking guild, USA

www.sunburyembroidery.co.uk
The Sunbury Embroidery Gallery, UK

www.vam.ac.uk
Victoria and Albert museum website, London, UK

FURTHER READING

4000 Flower & Plant Motifs: A Source Book by Graham Leslie McCallum, B T Batsford, 2005

Adventures in Needlework: Stitching with Passion by Jessica Aldred and Emily Peacock, Guild of Master Craftsman Publications, 2011

All that Glitters: Projects Featuring the Techniques of Goldwork and Stumpwork by Alison Cole, Search Press Ltd, 2007

Art of Embroidery: History of Style and Technique by Lanto Synge, Antique Collectors' Club Distribution, 2005

Contemporary Whitework by Tracy A. Franklin and Nicola Jarvis, Batsford, 2008

Embroidered Knot Gardens: Using Three-Dimensional Stumpwork, Canvas Work & Ribbon Work by Owen Davies and Gill Holdsworth, Batsford, 2006

The Embroidery Stitch Bible by Betty Barnden, Search Press, 2003

Goldwork Techniques, Projects & Pure Inspiration by Hazel Everett, Search Press, 2011

New Designs in Raised Embroidery by Barbara and Roy Hirst, Tuttle Publishing, 1999

New Ideas in Goldwork by Tracy A. Franklin, Batsford, 2008

A Perfect World in Ribbon Embroidery and Stumpwork by Di van Niekerk, Search Press, 2006

The Ribbon Embroidery Bible by Joan Gordon, Search Press, 2005

Royal School of Needlework Embroidery Techniques by Sally Saunders, Batsford Ltd, 2003

RSN Essential Stitch Guides, Search Press:
Blackwork by Becky Hogg (2011)
Canvas work by Rachel Doyle (2012)
Crewelwork by Jacqui McDonald (2011)
Goldwork by Helen McCook (2012)
Silk Shading by Sarah Homfray (2011)
Stumpwork by Kate Sinton (2011)
Whitework by Lizzy Lansberry (2012)

The Stitch Bible: A Comprehensive Guide to 225 Embroidery Stitches and Techniques by Kate Haxell, David and Charles, 2012

Tassel Making by Anna Crutchley, Apple Press, 2007

GLOSSARY

Aida
evenweave fabric with regularly spaced holes used for cross-stitch embroidery

appliqué
the application of fabric shapes to another fabric by hand stitching or fusing

Assisi work
counted-thread embroidery technique in which the background is worked in cross stitch with the motif left unstitched

Bargello
type of needlepoint that uses a long, straight stitch called "Florentine stitch," which forms a zigzag or flamelike pattern

basting
temporary stitching, usually a running stitch, used to keep fabrics in place while working; the basting stitches are removed once the work is finished; also known as tacking

batting
natural or synthetic padding material used for quilting; also known as wadding

beading needle
long, sharp, thin needle with a long eye used for sewing beads and sequins

beadloom
loom used for beadwork, which holds the threads so that you can create pieces of beading

beadwork
any type of surface decoration that uses beads and sequins

blackwork
counted-thread embroidery technique that is worked in small repeating patterns in black thread

Broderie anglaise
type of cutwork embroidery that creates small eyelet holes to form floral patterns; usually worked in white thread on white cotton fabric

canvas work
counted-thread embroidery technique worked on to an even canvas mesh

couching
attaching threads to a fabric by working evenly spaced stitches over the thread

counted thread work
any embroidery technique that requires you to count the threads and work symmetric patterns

crewelwork
type of embroidery worked with wools, traditionally on to a twill linen background

cutwork
either the name given to goldwork purls that are applied over soft string or when shapes of fabrics are cut out and the edges are either buttonholed or oversewn

digital machine embroidery
embroidery that is created by a digital machine; the user sets up the machine to work the piece

drawn thread work
embroidery technique where threads of fabric are removed and patterns are worked in the gaps

embroidery needle
needle with a sharp point and long eye

embroidery scissors
small, sharp pair of scissors used only for cutting threads

machine embroidery
embroidery that is worked by a sewing machine

mellor
laying tool used mostly in goldwork to smooth threads

metal threads
threads used in goldwork; they come in a range of types, including gold, silver, and copper

muslin
all-cotton woven fabric, known as calico in the UK

needlelace
stumpwork technique that creates pieces of lace made from thread and a needle; the stitches are variations of buttonhole stitch

pulled work
embroidery technique where the stitches are worked with a tight tension so that the fabric is manipulated to create patterns

quilting
stitching together layers of fabric, normally with a layer of batting or wadding in between

ribbon work
embroidery worked with silk ribbons, often used to create floral designs

ring frame
a frame normally made out of wood or plastic that is used to hold the fabric tight while stitching; also known as an embridery hoop

sewing thread
strong thread used for embroidery and securing fabric

smocking
embroidery that is worked on to pleated fabric to gather and manipulate it

smocking dots
dots marked on to a piece of paper, used as guides when sewing the fabric in patterns

smocking machine
machine used to pleat fabric so that smocking can be worked on to the pleated fabric

stiletto
tool used mainly in whitework for making a small hole in the fabric without breaking the threads

stranded cottons
embroidery threads that are sold in skeins; when cut there are six strands to sew with

surface embroidery
any embroidery technique that is worked on to a plain piece of fabric

stumpwork
embroidery that is raised to create a three-dimensional piece

tacking
temporary stitches to hold pieces of fabric together

thimble
often used to protect the fingers while stitching; normally made of metal or plastic

CONTRIBUTORS

Katy Aaberg
pipupeep@gmail.com
http://pipupeep.blogspot.com
flickr.com/photos/katiepipu
USA

Andrea Adams
beadmask@gmail.com
beadmask.com
USA

Jenny Adin-Christie
jenny.adin-christie@sky.com
UK

Kathi Alderink
sewcoolnurse@altelco.net
mylittlepeeps.etsy.com
USA

Haenni Annick
annick@haenni.info
haenni.info/blog/eclosion
Switzerland

Jo Avery
joave@btconnect.com
bearpawandbearpaw.blogspot.com
UK

Lucy Barter
lucy@forever-emb.com
USA

Gillian Bates
gillian_bates@hotmail.co.uk
gillian-bates.com
UK

Jazmin Berakha
jazminberakha@gmail.com
jazminberakha.com
Argentina

Susan Bischoff
susanbischoff@gmail.com
dollydelicacies.com
USA

Margaret Burns
brightburn@gmail.com
Canada

Trish Burr
erenvale@mweb.co.za
trishburr.co.za
South Africa

Fabienne Chabrolin
chabronico@free.fr
France

Mimi Chan
mxxmimi@hotmail.com
Hong Kong

Mary Corbet
mary@needlenthread.com
needlenthread.com
USA

Melissa Crowe
melissa.crowe@umpi.edu
checkoutgirlcrafts.blogspot.com
USA

Owen Davies
embroidery_textiles@hotmail.com
UK

Margaret Dier
margdier@yahoo.co.uk
UK

Rachel Doyle
rjdoyle@btopenworld.com
UK

**Peter and Penny Ellis
(Bluebells and Nightingales)**
welcome@bluebellsandnightingales.
co.uk
http://folksy.com/shops/
BluebellsandNightingales
UK

Tina Fitzpatrick
sewingseed@gmail.com
sewingseed.com
USA

Cécile Franconie
facile.cecile@yahoo.fr
facilececile.com
France

Eva Fulinova
tinctory@gmail.com
UK

Victoria Gertenbach
vgertenbach@yahoo.com
ruralretrodesigns.com
http://thesillyboodilly.blogspot.com
USA

Heather Gray (Modern Needleworks)
hkgray@comcast.net
modernneedleworks.com
USA

Sarah Greaves
greaves_s@yahoo.co.uk
sarahgreavesart.com
UK

Bec Groves
bec@becgroves.com
becgroves.com
Canada

Diana L. Grygo (The Lone Beader)
thelonebeader@gmail.com
thelonebeader.com
USA

Michala Gyetvai
michala.gyetvai@oneworld.com
michalagyetvai.co.uk
UK

Rita Hodge (Red Pepper Quilts)
redpepperquilts@gmail.com
redpepperquilts.com
Australia

Sarah Homfray
sarahhomfray@hotmail.com
UK

Nicola Hooper
nicola.hooper@yahoo.co.uk
UK

Emma How (Sampaguita Quilts)
eho16677@bigpond.net.au
http://sampaguitaquilts.blogspot.com
Australia

Sarah Johnson
remedynz@gmail.com
etsy.com/shop/remedynz
New Zealand

Zinaida Kazban
zkazban@gmail.com
http://hearty-craft.blogspot.com
UK

Gaby Vidlickova Kennedy
info@gabykennedy.com
UK

Terri King
tmkingfibers@gmail.com
USA

Monika Kinner-Whalen
mysweetprairie@gmail.com
mysweetprairie.blogspot.com
Canada

Judith Klausner
jgklausner@gmail.com
jgklausner.com
USA

**Corinne Kuhlmann-McHie
(September House)**
septemberhouse@hotmail.com
septemberhouse.etsy.com
USA

Lizzy Lansberry
lizzylansberry@hotmail.com
UK

David Lum (Lumme)
david@lumme.co.uk
lumme.co.uk

Emily Mackey (Maxemilia)
emily@maxemilia.com
maxemilia.com
USA

Lucy Margolius (Lucy Reed Designs)
info@lucyreeddesigns.com
UK

Maricor/Maricar
hi@maricormaricar.com
http://maricormaricar.com

Laura Mason
info@masonbee.co.uk
UK

Michelle Matthews
mi@michellematthews.com
michellematthews.com
USA

Joanne Melrose
jo.melrose@ntlworld.com
UK

Su Mwamba
tanglecrafts@ntlworld.com
tanglecrafts.co.uk
UK

Kirsty Neale
kirsty.neale@btinternet.com
kirstyneale.typepad.com
UK

Eva-Maria Nerling
e-nerling@gmx.de
Germany

Masako Newton
masakonewton@blueyonder.co.uk
UK

Niamh O'Connor (Urban Threads)
niamh@urbanthreads.com
USA

Harihi Okubo (CRESUS Artisanat)
cresusartisanat@cresus.org
http://cresus-parupi.blogspot.jp
Japan

Natalka Pavlysh
pavlysh@gmail.com
http://skrynka.blogspot.com
Ukraine

Emily Peacock
empeapod@yahoo.co.uk
emilypeacock.com
UK

Samantha Purdy
maudstitch@gmail.com
thepinpals.typepad.com
Canada

Lana Rabinovich
design@embroideryny.com
BelleCoccinelle.etsy.com
USA

Rebecca Ray
ralrayembroidery@hotmail.co.uk
ralrayembroidery.blogspot.com.au
Australia

Leisa Rich
monaleisa@bellshouth.net
USA

Julie Rofman
info@julierofmanjewelry.com
julierofmanjewelry.com
USA

Josie Rossington
follie_lincoln@yahoo.co.uk
follie.co.uk
UK

Karen Ruane
contemporaryembroidery@
hotmail.com
UK

Maki Saeki
info@roseberrys.net
roseberrys.net
Belgium

Esther Sanchez
Star-of-the-east@hotmail.com
http://StarBags.etsy.com
http://Starof theEast.etsy.com
Turkey

Kimberly Scola
chezsucrechez@gmail.com
chezsucrechez.com
USA

Heather Shaw (pi'lo)
heather@pilo.ca
pilo.ca
Canada

Kei Shinano
keishinano@gmail.com
Japan

Carol Shinn
cs@carolshinn.com
USA

Sophie Simpson (What Delilah Did)
sophie@whatdelilahdid.com
whatdelilahdid.com
UK

Viv Sliwka
viv_sliwka@hotmail.com
USA

Liz Smith
info@thestitchsmith.co.nz
thestitchsmith.co.nz
New Zealand

Megumi Sorita
sorita@nifty.com
Japan

Angela Souza (Magical Mystery Tuca)
weetuca@hotmail.com
magicalmysterytuca.etsy.com
Brasil

Estella Straatsma
Star-of-the-east@hotmail.com
http://StarBags.etsy.com
http://StaroftheEast.etsy.com
Turkey

Abigail Timmis
abigailtimmis@itwifi.net
http://abigailcecile.blogspot.com
USA

Eva Vercauteren
eva.vercauteren.telnet.be
thebluerabbithouse.com
Belgium

Amy Wallace
ovenfriedbeads@fuse.net
etsy.com/shop/ovenfriedbeads

Grace Walsh
gracewalsh4@gmail.com
UK

Hiromi Widerquist
harujiondesign@gmail.com
http://harujiondesign.blogspot.com
USA

Emily Wilmarth
emily@theflossbox.com
theflossbox.com
Sweden

TUTORIAL INDEX

INDEX

ACKNOWLEDGMENTS

- - - - - - - - - - - - - - - - - - -

A huge thank you to everyone who has contributed to this book. It was a privilege to write it, and I hope you enjoy reading and learning from it as much as I have enjoyed the writing and research.

Thank you to Lindy Dunlop and Isheeta Mustafi from RotoVision, and to Cath Senker, Rob Brandt, and Heidi Adnum for all of your patience and wisdom during the writing process. You have made this huge task such a great experience. Ann Roscoe: your assistance with the histories and background knowledge has been such a huge help—thank you. Megumi Sorita—thanks for all of your hard work with the translations.

Without my amazing tutors during my three-year apprenticeship at the Royal School of Needlework none of this would be possible, so I really do owe thanks to you. Those long hours and very sore fingers have been worthwhile! I'd like to give special thanks to Margaret Dier for all your help with this book.

I am also extremely grateful to Matthew Heaven, who has been a constant support, full of encouraging words and providing endless cups of tea and chocolate. Mabel the pug has sat with me through every minute of the process. And finally a massive thank you to my mum and sister for encouraging me to follow my heart and fulfil my dreams.

I dedicate this book to all of my family, friends, and students who know how important embroidery is to me. It means a lot to be able to share this love with you.